THE NEW TESTAMENT
AGAINST ITS
ENVIRONMENT

STUDIES IN BIBLICAL THEOLOGY

THE NEW TESTAMENT AGAINST ITS ENVIRONMENT

*The Gospel of Christ
the Risen Lord*

FLOYD V. FILSON

SCM PRESS LTD

BLOOMSBURY STREET LONDON

First published December 1950
Reprinted January 1952
Reprinted January 1953
Reprinted December 1954
Reprinted June 1956
Reprinted September 1959
Reprinted May 1963

Printed in Great Britain by
Northumberland Press Limited
Gateshead on Tyne

CONTENTS

FOREWORD

In April, 1949, Professor G. Ernest Wright and I gave the Haskell Lectures at Oberlin College, Oberlin, Ohio. We took as our subject 'The Bible Against Its Environment.' Professor Wright's three lectures were given under the subtitle, 'The God of Israel and the Gods of the Nations.' They contrasted the Old Testament with its environment by studies dealing successively with God, history, and the life of God's people. My own lectures, a study of the New Testament under the subtitle, 'The Gospel of Christ the Risen Lord,' took up in turn the same three themes. The question which I undertook to answer was: How far does the New Testament present a content which is distinct and different from non-Christian religious life and writings of New Testament times?

It may be asked why I stated the contrast between the New Testament and its environment in terms of 'The Gospel of Christ the Risen Lord.' In these words I tried to lay hold of the common and vital content of the entire New Testament. What is there in the New Testament which all the writers share, and which makes it legitimate to unite in a single collection these books by some dozen different authors? It is not difficult to answer this question. The New Testament undoubtedly has its common center in Jesus of Nazareth. It tells a story about him, and the point of the story is that he was the Christ of Israel, sent of God to carry out God's climactic purpose for his people. That story reaches a climax, but not an end, in the Resurrection. While some modern theologies and gospel hymns seem to suggest that the Cross marked the end and completion of the work of Jesus Christ, the New Testament speaks with quite another accent. The crucified Jesus was raised from the dead, elevated to a place of unique honor and authority with God, and is now the risen Lord of his people. This converging of thought on Jesus as God's central agent, as the Christ of Israel who was crucified but is now the risen Lord, is common to all New Testament writers. It is not only common; it is basic in their worship and thinking. If, therefore, we are to speak faithfully concerning the New Testament and its environment, we must focus our attention chiefly upon this common and basic theme; we must ask whether this is something distinct and unique, or whether it is history's crowning instance of successful plagiarism or anemic eclecticism.

CHAPTER ONE

'THE GOD AND FATHER OF OUR LORD JESUS CHRIST'

THE New Testament message concerning God speaks continually of 'the God and Father of our Lord Jesus Christ' (2 Cor. 1.3; Eph. 1.3; 1 Pet. 1.3). What it has to say concerning God is vitally linked with the teaching and work of Jesus, to whom God was unquestionably the central reality and for whom prayer to God as Father was so significant that his Aramaic word for Father, *Abba*, lived on even in the Greek tradition and in the prayer life of the Church (Mark 14.36; Rom. 8.15; Gal. 4.6).[1] In the minds of the New Testament writers, theism is interlocked with Christology. Statements concerning God contain a reference, expressed or implied, to the person and work of Jesus Christ. Therefore we can grasp the distinctive character of the New Testament message concerning God only by clear discernment of the originality of its teaching about Jesus Christ.

I

To discuss this or any other theme in relation to the New Testament's environment requires us to consider both Judaism and the Hellenistic world. The logical method is to consider first the relation to Judaism. At once we note the large extent of common ground. This close relation was not due merely to the fact that both Judaism and New Testament Christianity possessed the Old Testament, although this in itself insured a great area of agreement. It was due also to the fact that Judaism, as it existed in the days of Jesus and the Apostles,

[1] Cf. G. Kittell, in *Theologisches Wörterbuch zum N.T.*, Vol. I, 1933, pp. 4-6; G. Dalman, *The Words of Jesus*, 1909, pp. 189 ff.; T. W. Manson, *The Teaching of Jesus*, 1931, p. 50.

had other points of contact with what we know to be New Testament teaching. To take but one significant example, the expectation of the Resurrection, although not unchallenged in Jewish circles, was widely held (cf. Acts 23.8) and constituted a point of relation between the New Testament and Judaism which cannot be explained by common use of the Old Testament, where the expectation is but rarely found.[2]

To state the area of agreement more nearly, it must be noted, as we implied in the reference to the Resurrection, that the most vital features of agreement in thought and outlook were with the Pharisees. The New Testament shows no vital kinship with the priestly Sadducees.[3] Nor were the militant and nationalistic Zealots any more closely related to the earliest stages of Christianity; Solomon Zeitlin's amazing attempt[4] to characterize the earliest apostolic period as one of political aim and interest is a curious but glaring mistake. Moreover, while Jesus has been described as an Essene, the way in which he went to the people and lived in free association with them makes the description entirely unconvincing (Matt. 11.19; Mark 2.15 f.; Luke 15.1 f.).[5] The one party or sect of Judaism with which he had the greatest agreement in items of religious thought

[2] E. F. Sutcliffe, in *The O.T. and the Future Life*, 1946, stressed that the O.T. expected survival in Sheol, but concedes that the life there is pictured in ' almost entirely negative' terms (p. 190).

[3] It is clear from Jesus' words in Mark 1.44, 11.17, as well as from his deep concern for Jerusalem (Matt. 23.37), that he did not deny the role of the priests in the life of Israel. But the center of his worship and thought was not in sacrifice and ritual; these were secondary (Matt. 5.23 f.; Mark 2.26; Luke 10.31 f.) and dispensable (Mark 13.2). With the political opportunism of the Sadducees he had no sympathy.

[4] In *Who Crucified Jesus?*, 1942, pp. 180 ff. For an attempt to prove that Jesus was a political revolutionist, see R. Eisler, *The Messiah Jesus and John the Baptist*, Eng. tr., 1931. He has been answered by J. W. Jack, *The Historic Christ*, 1933. Simon the Cananaean or Zealot must be a disciple who *had been* a Zealot (Mark 3.18; Luke 6.15), or was of impetuous character.

[5] So M. Goguel, *Life of Jesus*, Eng. tr., 1933, pp. 262 f.; Ch. Guignebert, *Jesus*, Eng. tr., 1935, p. 400. For information on the Essenes see J. Klausner, *Jesus of Nazareth*, Eng. tr., 1925, pp. 201 f., 206 ff., 244 f.

was the Pharisee group.[6] It is therefore of the greatest importance that in recent decades the position of the Pharisees has become much better known through the writings of such scholars as C. G. Montefiore,[7] I. Abrahams,[8] R. T. Herford,[9] G. F. Moore,[10] and J. Klausner.[11] The positive strength of the Pharisaic viewpoint is now much better known to us than it was known in any previous Christian century.

The more we thus come to know the Judaism of the first century, and especially the Pharisaism of that time, the more acute our problem becomes. Jesus and Paul and the other apostolic leaders were Jews. We cannot understand them unless we possess a vivid sense of their deep indebtedness to their Jewish heritage and environment. They willingly and gratefully lived their lives in the framework of the Judaism of their day. The misguided Nazi racial pride which tried to make of Jesus an Aryan cannot appeal to any person who knows the New Testament.[12] Jesus was a Jew; Peter was a Jew; Paul was a Jew. Moreover, almost all of the writers of the New

[6] The Jewish group represented in the 'Zadokite Work,' which R. H. Charles, *Apocrypha and Pseudepigrapha of the O.T.*, Vol. II, pp. 787 ff., dates between 18 B.C. and A.D. 70, and C. C. Torrey, *The Apocryphal Literature*, 1945, p. 128, dates not earlier than the first century A.D., is too little known to help us here. It coupled priestly origin, prophetic interest, and Messianic expectation. The new 'Sectarian Document' discovered in the 'Ain Feshka cave near the northern end of the Dead Sea is little known as yet, though its pre-Christian date, defended ably by W. F. Albright and S. A. Birnbaum in the October, 1949, number of the *Bulletin of the American Schools of Oriental Research*, will assure it careful study. M. Burrows describes its contents briefly in *The Biblical Archaeologist* for September, 1948, pp. 58-60.

[7] See especially *The Synoptic Gospels*, 2 vols., 2nd ed., 1927; *The O.T. and After*, 1923.

[8] *Studies in Pharisaism and the Gospels*, 2 vols., 1917 and 1924.

[9] Especially in *The Pharisees*, 1924.

[10] *Judaism in the First Centuries of the Christian Era: The Age of the Tannaim*, 3 vols., 1927-30.

[11] Especially in *Jesus of Nazareth*.

[12] E. Tanner, *The Nazi Christ*, 1942, is an effective critique of Nazi errors.

Testament were Jews. Should anyone conclude that more Gentile authors shared in the writing of the New Testament than the traditional one, namely, Luke, the situation only becomes the more striking, for in spite of the inclusion of one or more Gentiles among the authors, the environmental connection of the New Testament as a whole is prevailingly Jewish. This is not a Gentile book. Its deepest ties are with Judaism, and indeed with Palestinian and Pharisaic Judaism rather than with the Hellenistic Judaism which we associate with Philo of Alexandria.[13]

All of this only sharpens the issue which we now have to face: Is there anything in the New Testament which is inherently and inevitably irreconcilable with first-century Judaism?

To this question more than one voice in our time has returned a negative answer. They say that there is no necessary clash between Judaism and the Christianity which comes to us from Jesus.[14] Such scholars identify certain features of the New Testament as later and distorting additions to the teaching of Jesus, and they hold or imply that Christians should discard these additions in order to be true to what Jesus really represented and what Judaism would then be ready to accept. This answer is not confined to Jews.[15] It comes from a number of Christian scholars. What are we to say to this solution?

[13] Points of contact with Hellenistic Judaism do occur, and we must not overlook the substantial agreement between Palestinian and Hellenistic Judaism, but the influence of the LXX and of Philo are not determinative of the basic content. Note, for example, that N.T. Scripture quotation reflects the Palestinian Canon. H. A. Wolfson, in *Philo*, 2 vols., 1947, has erred in declaring that Philo shaped the thinking of Christianity from the outset; see my review of Wolfson's significant work, in *Jewish Quarterly Review*, XXXIX, pp. 97-102.

[14] See, e.g., the statements of D. W. Riddle in *Jesus and the Pharisees*, 1928, Part III.

[15] This deletion of accretions is by no means sufficient to satisfy all Jews. Klausner, for instance, *op. cit.*, p. 414, finds the ethical code of Jesus so wrapped in 'miracles and mysticism,' which means Christology, that he feels compelled to charge Jesus with an attempt to shatter Judaism and its idea of God (pp. 378 ff.).

It is pertinent to say that the possibility of such easy agreement never occurred to the first-century leaders of Judaism. We have recognized the areas of agreement between Jesus and Pharisees; but it still remains true, as James Parkes, for example, clearly states,[16] that the Jewish leaders vigorously rejected the challenge and claim of Jesus. Define that claim as you will, they rejected it; on this point the New Testament and every available ancient Jewish witness agree. With equal decisiveness they refused to have anything to do with the apostolic message.[17] If we let the attitude of the first-century Jewish representatives settle the matter, we must say that they found something in Jesus with which they could not make peace and still hold to their traditional position. There was significant difference, which no amount of friendly modern apologetic and diplomacy can gloss over. If, then, it was the conviction of both the Jewish leaders and the New Testament writers that a significant and even radical opposition existed, we had better recognize the fact and seek to determine wherein lies the reason for the open break.

II

As we undertake to state the ground of difference, one observation is needed. We do violence to the content of the New Testament if we consent to carry on the study as though the issue were merely a matter of comparing ideas. Since the religious man has a mind, he is indeed under obligation to think, and hence to state in the clearest possible manner the nature and content of his faith. But religion is far more than

[16] *Judaism and Christianity*, 1948, p. 70.
[17] Acts 6.7 indicates that there were exceptions, whom Charles, *op. cit.*, p. 786, would seek among the Zadokite group; see Note 6 above. The statement in Acts must not be given too sweeping a reference. In this connection it is interesting to recall the ancient tradition that the Beloved Disciple was of priestly origin.

a collection of ideas. A living religion deals with God and his action, not merely with man's ideas. It has an organic unity which represents the relation to God in the total range of faith and life.

Failure to do justice to this fact makes some books on our subject pitifully inadequate. Take, for example, the already mentioned recent book by James Parkes on *Judaism and Christianity*. Parkes is a professing Christian, of the Anglican Church. He discusses the relation between Jesus and the first-century Jews by comparing Jesus as a teacher with the teachers of the Pharisees. As he examines the ideas which Jesus and his opponents held, he feels that both sides had justification and so were justified in continuing along separate lines. He specifically excludes from this particular discussion such questions as who Jesus in fact was, what authorization he had from God the Father, and what the significance of his life and death was. He does not see in the Resurrection anything which might prove decisive as to the right of Judaism to continue. There are good points on both sides. Therefore let Judaism, which is the modern development of Pharisaism, and Christianity, which in a garbled and misleading way preserves the teaching of Jesus, both go on until we find the truth which neither fully has; only then are we to join in a union which uses what both groups have to offer. So Parkes argues.

It is impossible to find basic consistency in this position. Parkes professes to hold to the Incarnation and Atonement, but when he compares Jesus with the Pharisees, he does not find these things relevant. 'Both religions are true.'[18] These things are in the New Testament, and the New Testament writers plainly thought that both Jews and Gentiles should accept them

---

[18] *Op. cit.*, p. 19. How Parkes can think these doctrines true for Gentiles and irrelevant for Jews I do not understand. Peter, Paul, and the numerous other Jews of the Apostolic Church evidently would not understand either. Parkes implies that they were in the wrong group and had wrong ideas.

and shape their life accordingly. Yet Parkes, while holding these beliefs in the twentieth century, does not seem to think they were relevant for first-century Jews. The limitation of the discussion to a comparison of teaching ideas has led to an inconsistent and indefensible position. The best method, the only sound method, is to start with the clear decision of the opponents of Jesus and the Apostles. We must recognize that a personal claim of Jesus, clearly attested and accepted in the New Testament and reflected in garbled form in Jewish sources,[19] endangered the continuation of the Judaism to which Jesus came. We cannot make sense of either Jewish opposition or Christian procedure unless we start with this fact.

This does not mean that Jesus disowned or abandoned Judaism. Neither he nor his followers did that. They held rather that they offered the true Judaism. They knew that the acceptance of their position meant the radical transformation of the Judaism in which they lived, and this meant that the recognized Jewish leaders would be immediately and vitally affected by such changes.[20] The intent of Jesus and the Apostles, however, was not to destroy or abandon Judaism, but rather to act under God the Father in bringing the ancestral faith to its truest and climactic form. In one sense, to be sure, the separation may be blamed on Jesus and the Christian group, since they pressed a claim which required either a transformation of existing official and institutional Judaism or an ejection of the Christian spokesmen. But in another sense the decision was made by the Jewish leaders, and only their negative position toward Christ (Mark 14.64; Acts 4.5 f.), a position finally shared by the majority of the people and expressed in acts which drove the

[19] See R. T. Herford, *Christianity in Talmud and Midrash*, 1903.
[20] The note of fulfilment (Mark 1.15; Matt. 5.17) means that all Jewish thought and prophecy must be related to the message and work of Jesus. The eschatological note means that all Jewish life and institutions must be adjusted to the incipient final action of God through Jesus. The claim of Jesus calls for a loyal response of all Jews, and especially the leaders, to his teaching and leadership.

followers of Jesus out of the synagogue (Acts 6.9-14, 8.1, 9.20-25, 13.45, etc.), resulted in a separate Christian Church. The clash was real, but it was a clash within the bounds of Judaism as long as the Jewish leaders permitted it to stay there.[21] Not even the inclusion of the Gentiles in the Apostolic Church meant the abandonment of the Christians' claim to be the true Judaism. The conflict first took shape within the Jewish framework.

The difference thus must be seen first within the Jewish framework, and it centered in the claim that Christ acted for God in so central and decisive a way that as a result all individual and group life must be shaped and all theology regarded from this Christo-centric position.

What the New Testament has to say about God, then, is involved in what it has to say concerning Jesus and what he did. He announced the climactic and decisive action of God (Matt. 12.28; Mark 1.15, 9.1, 14.62). He claimed to speak with authority on behalf of God (Matt. 5.22,28, etc.; Mark 8.38). He assumed the right to interpret the meaning of Scripture and he particularly rejected the authority of the oral tradition (Matt. 5.21 f., 27 f., 33-37; Mark 7.6-9). To grasp the extent of the difference between Jesus and the Pharisees we must remember that to the latter the Torah was not simply the Pentateuch. The tradition which had taken form, the 'tradition of the elders,' was for the Pharisee as much a part of God's revealed will as was the written law itself.[22] But Jesus rejected this tradition. Moreover, he took upon himself the right to interfere in the conduct of the temple concessions (Mark 11.15 f.). He claimed a role which Pharisees and priests could accept only if they were

---

[21] The Jewish framework of the Christian movement is clear not only from the frequently reflected conviction of the disciples that they rightly worship in Temple (Acts 3.1, 21.26) and synagogue (Acts 6.9, 9.20, 13.14, 18.4), but also from the access which the Judaizers have to largely Gentile churches, which do not regard the presentation of the claims of legalistic Judaism as utterly alien to their own heritage as Christians.

[22] See Moore, *op. cit.*, Vol. I, pp. 253 f.

willing to grant him a position superior to and independent of them.

III

Who could make such a commanding claim? One answer, which in any case is part of the truth, is that he was a prophet of God. Indeed, he so described himself (Mark 6.4), and we know that not only by his disciples but also in popular view he was openly regarded as a prophet (Mark 6.14 f., 8.28; Matt. 21.11). It is clear, however, that the early Church from its very beginning explicitly regarded him as the fulfilment of the Jewish Messianic expectation. Form criticism as well as the study of the speeches of Acts support the plain testimony of the Gospels that Jesus was so regarded from the first days of the Church.[23] This conclusion may be taken as established. Yet it was not a natural deduction from the fact of the Crucifixion; rather, the reverse was true. Critical scholarship, however, has failed to produce any explanation of this unanimous affirmation of the Apostolic Church which can effectively compete with the New Testament explanation, namely, that the Church regarded Jesus as Messiah, and the authorities condemned Jesus as a Messianic pretender, because a personal claim was inherent in his own outlook.[24] To be sure, we must discard decisively the Fourth Gospel's dramatic picture that Jesus was clearly recognized as Messiah, and openly admitted the role, from the earliest

[23] Form criticism seeks the home of the gospel tradition in the worshipping, i.e., Christ-centered, community. On the significance of the speeches of Acts for the earliest, 'pre-Pauline' Church, see C. H. Dodd, *The Apostolic Preaching and Its Developments*, 1937.

[24] This is pointedly asserted by B. S. Easton, *Christ in the Gospels*, 1930, p. 171. He rightly states that since 'God's initial act has been performed' and 'manifested in the work of Jesus' (p. 163), the imminent Kingdom is beginning; this decisive action of God in Jesus is thus a strong argument for the Messianic identification.

17

part of his public ministry.[25]   We must further recognize that when Jesus accepted the role, he put his own discriminating interpretation upon it.[26]   But the sound conclusion from all the New Testament evidence is that he saw in his ministry the fulfil-ment of the deepest expectations of his people, that he so agreed when his disciples finally voiced this conclusion, and that he was put to death by an unwarranted twisting of this claim into a charge of rebellious political ambition.

To reject this conclusion is to require, in addition to a radical discounting of the Gospels and of the intelligence or honesty of the earliest Christians, a further threefold improbability: first, it implies that Jesus assumed a unique and commanding role with no adequate decision as to what his own place in God's movement was; second, it accuses the opponents of trumping up a totally unfounded charge on the basis of which to effect his execution;[27] and third, it is forced to assume that while neither Jesus nor the disciples saw reason to identify him as Messiah during his lifetime, once the fact of his official rejection and humiliating crucifixion was added to the picture they immediately leaped to the identification.   This does not make sense.   The view that there was a real basis for the Messianic identification in the ministry and thinking of Jesus can claim to be far the more simple and convincing historical conclusion. In my view it is theological presuppositions rather than historical data which to some have made this conclusion appear untenable.

[25] Chap. I contains every significant Christological designation which this Gospel is written to present: Logos, God, Lamb of God, Messiah, Christ, Son of God, King of Israel, Son of Man. This concentration of titles so early is dramatic rather than chronological.

[26] This reinterpretation is contained in the temptation narrative (Matt. 4.1-11), which correctly reflects Jesus' later teaching, and in the passion predictions and their later amplification.   On the latter passages, see V. Taylor, *Jesus and His Sacrifice*, 1937.

[27] The charge as formulated in Luke 23.2 is suspect in so far as the evangelists, including Luke (20.25), agree that Jesus disappointed the Zealots and avoided rebellious teaching concerning tribute.   But its political twist to the Messianic claim is convincing; only on political grounds would Pilate act.

This recognition of the unique role of Jesus was—not originated, but rather—confirmed by the Resurrection. Once his disciples were convinced that Jesus had been raised from the dead and given the place of honor and authority by God, his decisive role and right to command were placed beyond question. The Messiah is not merely one of a number of political candidates for man's sovereign suffrage. Jesus the Christ is Lord. R. Travers Herford[28] has the misguided statement, and Parkes[29] shares the attitude with him, that the 'only' thing which divided the Pharisees and the early Christians was the fact that to the Christians Jesus was the Messiah. But this is one of those cases in which one absolutely basic and decisive fact determines the whole life loyalty. It claims and organizes and controls life. To call it the 'only' difference is a sad failure to grasp the significance of this life-shaping choice for or against the claim of Jesus.

Thus far we have defined the difference between the Pharisees and Jesus by pointing out the personal claim of Jesus. This is not a sufficient statement of the situation. It might be understood to imply that this was only a claim of a man with whom other men might justifiably disagree. The full truth excludes this possibility. As we have implied in what has been said, the message and claim of both Jesus and the Apostolic Church was that in what he said and did, God himself was definitely active to bring his providential purpose to fulfilment. God sent him; God was acting in and through him; God was doing something which called for a response of faith and acceptance. God did this within Judaism. He made his offer and claim first of all to Judaism.[30] He did so uniquely and authoritatively in Jesus. There is not the slightest evidence that Jesus ever thought of

[28] *The Pharisees*, p. 212.
[29] *Op. cit.*, p. 72.
[30] The order which Paul saw in God's working and himself followed : 'to the Jew first' (Rom. 1.16), was in fact expressed in Jesus' direct and persistent appeal to his own people. He rarely leaves Palestine proper, and then never for a public ministry. It is interesting to note that when

himself as only one of a democratic band of spokesmen for God. He is represented as speaking with a note of authority and urgency in keeping with the unique and climactic role which it was given him to play. And beyond all possibility of question his disciples firmly held that he occupied a place above them and stood in a unique relation to God's action and purposes.

That is why I have entitled this chapter ' The God and Father of our Lord Jesus Christ.' In this New Testament expression we have the heart of the common New Testament conviction concerning God and the relation of Jesus to God. What God has done in Jesus is the most important thing which men can know. It is the way we sufficiently know God and his work and will. It involves so close a link between Jesus and his Father that only a high Christology will adequately express what we know of God and what we should think of Christ.

I know that men can reject this entire message which is so prominent, clear, and urgent in the New Testament. But I cannot understand how men can say that this is not a vitally fresh message, or that the New Testament is not emphatic about it. This Gospel says that in Christ God has acted as never before and with effective power to carry his purpose to climactic fulfilment, and that since this message, by its very nature and content, permits no neutrality, God's action in Christ calls for a response of faith and loyalty. Moreover, it is not a merely borrowed message. It presents the Messiah not in inherited Jewish fashion,[31] but in an original form which derives from

Jesus heals a Gentile, the Gospels—written when the Church had become largely Gentile and Gentile contacts on Jesus' part would have been of practical use in teaching and controversy—tell us that the healings were performed at a distance.

[31] Christian teaching concerning fulfilment of the Old Testament must not think in terms of exact, literal correspondence between promise and realization. A. C. Zenos, *The Plastic Age of the Gospel*, 1927, p. 12, makes this point. Even the first-century Jewish Messianic expectation was far from rigid, and this allowed for reinterpretation.

the unique implications of the ministry, resurrection, and Lordship of Christ. In its essential core it is there from the first of the Apostolic Age, and so early an origin finds convincing explanation only in the corresponding mind and action of Jesus himself.

IV

From this point of view it is possible to consider whether the idea of God in the New Testament presents anything new in relation to the Old Testament and Judaism. The fact that Jesus met opposition, that Jewish leaders moved to exclude him from further ministry (Mark 3.6, 11.28, 14.1 f.), and that his followers encountered active hostility in one place after another, can only indicate that Judaism sensed a message which was not identical with the prevailing theology.[32] Although the question of leadership was directly involved, the clash cannot be explained as a mere rivalry for ecclesiastical preferment. It had a theological basis. The leaders of Judaism did not find an authoritative divine word in Jesus' humble ministry and disturbing reinterpretation of the divine Scripture. Above all, this Judaism could not see a revelation of God, of the divine nature and purpose, in the Cross and the Resurrection. The New Testament takes the opposite position; the career and claim of Christ are interlocked with the content of theology. Moreover, the ministry, teaching, and death of Jesus are of one piece. That the holy God is not only the God of suffering love but also and specifically the seeking Father is the New Testament theology,[33] and the violence

[32] The hostility of the Sadducees, manifested only when Jesus had cleansed the temple, may have grown out of considerations of prestige, profit, and political expediency more than theological understanding, but the Pharisees evidently reacted early and often against the teaching and implicit claim of Jesus.

[33] See R. Otto's quotations from other scholars and his own conclusion in *The Kingdom of God and the Son of Man*; Eng. tr., 1938, pp. 393 ff.

with which the Jews rejected this view in the person of Jesus and in the preaching of the Apostles underlines the fact that there was something in the Christian idea of God which Judaism did not parallel.

This does not mean that Jesus and the New Testament writers disowned the Old Testament. On the contrary, they quoted it, alluded to it, and found in it their one great source of religious vocabulary and concepts.[34] They often appealed from the official Judaism of their day to the Scripture, the fulfilment of whose deepest themes they found in the fresh work of God in their time. Yet the slowness of the disciples to see in Christ's rejection and suffering the work and revelation of God,[35] and the prevailing lack of any contemporary Jewish parallel to the doctrine of the Cross,[36] indicate that the Scripture, without the explicit action of God in Christ, was not clear enough and decisive enough to render the career of Christ and the apostolic interpretation of it superfluous or unimportant.

In the new message a fresh, vital, basic, theological content was embodied. It is not merely that Jesus and the New Testament leave out of view the dull, dismal, and unreal areas which make up so much of apocalyptic speculation and rabbinical

W. Manson argues in *Jesus the Messiah*, 1943, pp. 98 ff., 171 ff., that Jesus' fusion and synoptic use of the concepts Davidic Messiah, Servant of the Lord, and Heavenly Son of Man had a rich preparation in the O.T. and pre-Christian Judaism. Yet, although Manson goes beyond what some scholars would concede, he too explicitly states the originality of Jesus.

[34] The evidence is given in considerable detail in R. V. G. Tasker, *The Old Testament in the New Testament*, 1946.

[35] The Gospels, by their report that the disciples could not accept the necessity of the Cross (Mark 8.32, 9.32), make clear that Christ's career was far more than a simple expression of what they already understood and expected. This is true on any critical view of these passages.

[36] The second Messianic figure, the suffering Son of Joseph, appears later in rabbinical tradition, but no evidence attests the existence or prevalence of this expectation in the days of Jesus. As Moore, *op. cit.*, Vol. II, p. 370, suggests, it was hardly an absolutely new conception at the time of the first extant mention of it.

elaboration.[37] This omission in itself is significant; I know of no truly great religious literature which does not carry the marks of simplicity and concentration. To select and concentrate upon what really matters, to have what Moffatt's rendering of a New Testament phrase so well expresses, 'a sense of what is vital' (Phil. 1.10), is indeed of the utmost importance. But this is not all; in the area in which the New Testament concentrates there is a penetration, a clear and authoritative word about the gracious action of the holy God, a theology in which the Cross is the natural symbol of the seeking love of God and in which the Resurrection is the interpreting focus of the triumphant Lordship of God.

This message finds a true foundation and prelude in the Old Testament,[38] but it cannot be set down as merely another statement of what is equally clear and effective in that earlier form. When God acts decisively he gives to those of faith a climactic revelation, in the light of which all else is to be interpreted and understood. Theology strictly understood finds its basic and constant material in the action and person of the God and Father of our Lord Jesus Christ. This is the New Testament presentation of God. It did not come from its environment. It is either an original human delusion or a fresh, climactic revelation.

[37] This is a point which 'anthologies' of rabbinical and other Jewish writings tend to obscure.

[38] The O.T. history tells of the earlier stages of the action of this same God. The Cross finds a preparation not merely in the Suffering Servant figure of Second Isaiah, but also in the suffering leaders of Israel, especially the prophets (cf. Heb. 11.32-40), and in the suffering of the chosen people, for the repeated statement that Israel suffered for her sins does not obscure the fact that her pagan neighbors often enjoyed undeserved power and privileges and her election proved to be a door not to privilege but to costly service of God. The resurrection has a fainter background in the Old Testament, but in addition to unmistakable expressions (Isa. 26.19; Dan. 12.2) and predictions of lesser clarity (e.g. Ps. 16.10, 73.24; Job 19.25 ff. is not so clear as often supposed), the renewal or restoration of Israel is a promise which offers possibilities of later personal application (e.g. Ezek. 37; Hos. 6.2).

V

As we pointed out early in our discussion, to compare the New Testament with Judaism is but half of our task. Christianity lived almost from the first in active touch with the Hellenistic world. Indeed, it is highly probable that even during the ministry of Jesus Greek-speaking Jews were among his followers. It is the serious error of C. C. Torrey to make no allowance for this probability and to ignore the undeniable evidence which the Stephen-Barnabas group in the Jerusalem Church provides that the Church was bilingual from the earliest days.[39]

The wide use of the Septuagint[40] and the continual stream of pilgrims to Jerusalem are a reminder that more Jews lived in Gentile lands than in Palestine, and while it would be foolish to think that mere residence in Gentile lands indicated widespread abandonment of Jewish faith and practices, it certainly is true that either by way of active defenses, as in the case of Paul and his father (Phil. 3.5; cf. Acts 23.6), or by way of accommodation, such as we see in the attempted synthesis of Philo and the much less loyal syncretism in Asia Minor,[41] the Jews of the Dispersion had to recognize and relate themselves to the Gentile world.

The contact with Gentiles and Hellenistic life, however, was not merely a Dispersion matter. Not only were the representatives of the foreign ruling power present in Palestine, but the Decapolis and various other Greek cities there remind us that the relation to Hellenistic life was a Palestinian problem as well. The role of Palestine as a border region on the Roman Empire's eastern frontier, and the ties of Palestinian Jews with their

[39] See my book, *Pioneers of the Primitive Church*, 1940, pp. 52 ff.

[40] Its role in the Dispersion and among Christians is discussed in my article on 'The Septuagint and the New Testament,' in *The Biblical Archaeologist* for May, 1946.

[41] Paul's letter to the Colossians is one witness to such a syncretistic trend in Asia Minor.

countrymen in the Parthian Empire, especially in Mesopotamia, further sharpened the attention of thoughtful Jews to the presence of the Hellenistic life which for centuries had been reaching into Palestine from the west, north, and south-west. Indeed, the Jews themselves had been divided into opposed camps, and a civil war, more or less thinly veiled, had continued, first under the Syrians and then under the Romans, between the assimilationist and the separatist Jews. It was a live problem in Jesus' day, and the Hellenistic architecture of the Temple and of other great structures in Jerusalem and Palestine, as well as the openness of the leading Sadducees towards Hellenistic culture, accentuate the fact that Hellenistic life had established a militant but precarious beachhead in Palestine in the first century.[42] Christianity took its rise and determined the geographical direction of its spread in the time when this beachhead offered the essential conditions of a westward expansion.

The Christian movement, therefore, never lived an hour in a region which was purely Jewish. To be sure, Jesus was a Jew. He may have spoken a little Greek; that seems *a priori* likely, and must often have been true of a resident of Galilee. He may have had occasional contacts with Gentiles during his ministry; the Gospel indications to that effect are entirely credible. But it cannot be seriously questioned that he was a Jew, speaking Aramaic as his usual teaching medium (cf. Mark 5.41, 7.34, 14.36, 15.34),[43] and loyal to his Jewish heritage and setting.[44] Moreover, the earliest disciples were Jewish, and it was only by a gradual process that they saw and accepted a wider role in the Gentile world.[45] Nevertheless, even in Palestine the Chris-

[42] See G. E. Wright and F. V. Filson, *Westminster Historical Atlas to the Bible*, 1945, pp. 83-86.

[43] The Aramaic word in Mark 7.34 is said to have been spoken in the Decapolis region (v. 31)!

[44] See note 30. Cf. Matt. 23.37.

[45] It is clear from both Acts and the letters of Paul that the trend to explicit universalism was vigorously opposed within the Church itself, and only gradually attained full expression.

tian group had common ground with the Hellenistic world. In language and its accompanying contacts the wider world was with the Primitive Church from the first, and while the contacts were certainly meager at first, they grew as the movement expanded. This was natural and necessary; no religious group can grow without sharing the media of communication and the framework of life with those to whom they go. They dare not surrender to that framework in all its phases; but they cannot work if they are totally alien to it.

The common ground with the Hellenistic world was inevitable, and it was not long before the prevailing environment of the Christian Church was Gentile. What does the New Testament indicate of the Christian way of dealing with that non-Christian environment, especially in regard to faith in God and teaching concerning him?

One general observation ought to be made at the outset. The primary kinship of the New Testament is not with this Gentile environment, but rather with the Jewish heritage and environment of which we spoke in the first half of this lecture. We often are led by our traditional creeds and theology to think in terms dictated by Gentile and especially Greek concepts. We know that not later than the second century there began the systematic effort of the Apologists to show that the Christian faith perfected the best in Greek philosophy. We are aware, too, that scholars have pointed out aspects of New Testament thought which are akin to Greek thinking.[46] The recovery of a better understanding of first-century Judaism, however, and a more careful study of the New Testament must block any trend to regard the New Testament as a group of documents expressive of the Gentile mind. This book's kinship is primarily and overwhelmingly with Judaism and the Old Testament. The

[46] W. R. Halliday, *The Pagan Background of Early Christianity*, 1925, gives a good survey of the Gentile background. P. E. Moore, in *The Christ of the N. T.*, 1924, and *Christ the Word*, 1927, sees kingship with ' the Greek tradition.'

criticisms of a Celsus that the Christians did not really 'belong' to the Roman world of their day contained truth.[47] We may make the mistake of thinking that the Church was at home in the Gentile world, but both the Early Church and its opponents knew better. The New Testament speaks always with disapproval and usually with blunt denunciation of Gentile cults and philosophies. It agrees essentially with the Jewish indictment of the pagan world.

VI

I know the one chief objection which may be made to this statement. It may be charged that I am ignoring the difference between the earliest years of the Church, the earliest years especially of the Aramaic-speaking Church, and the shortly subsequent development which made something quite different of the new faith. It may be said that there was once a group of disciples who had a simple faith framed in a truly Jewish setting, but that in some way which is not too clear—I have never seen a really successful attempt to conceal the gap in the argument right at this point—in some way, the faith got loose and was launched in the Gentile world, where it became a quite different thing and developed into something which Jesus and his first disciples would not have recognized or approved. It may be claimed that philosophy, mystery ideas, and social and cult practices alien to the initial movement so transformed the faith that what resulted is actually the product of the Hellenistic world. This is the real issue: Did the appearance of essential aspects of the New Testament faith come only after the original form had been radically altered by forces which were clearly and distinctly Hellenistic?

[47] His attack, as reported in Origen's work *Against Celsus*, pointed out that the Christians refused, in his view wrongly, to take part in the pagan, polytheistic life of the Empire.

It would be wrong to deal lightly with this objection. It is not enough to say that if the original faith had no real message to the Gentile world, the historian will have a hard time saying why it invaded the Gentile world so soon and so effectively. This is a relevant observation but not a complete answer. Nor is it sufficient to deride the Gentile world for suffering so great a 'failure of nerve'[48] that it grasped in desperation at a quite unsuitable faith, only to find that it must immediately reconstruct that faith out of Gentile resources. We must offer a more careful discussion of the real question: Is the New Testament the product of a secondary phase of Christian development which has not merely obscured but even warped the true original message? Did the essential New Testament content take its rise in the Gentile world, or did it come to the Gentile world as a gift and a challenge, an indictment and an answer to need?

Discussion has often gone astray because the question has been wrongly asked. We do not ask whether the New Testament, written in Greek,[49] reflects Gentile thought and life. It does, of course, and as we have said, it was inevitable that such should be the case. Nor do we ask whether we find in the philosophy and religion of the earlier Gentile world parallels to certain terms and ideas of the New Testament. There are such

[48] This expression has been made common coin by Gilbert Murray. See *Five Stages of Greek Religion*, 1925.

[49] It would be much easier to demonstrate the N.T.'s basic independence of Gentile influence if the Aramaic origin of one Gospel (C. F. Burney, *The Aramaic Origin of the Fourth Gospel*, 1922) or of all Gospels (C. C. Torrey, *The Four Gospels*, 1933; *Our Translated Gospels*, 1936) or of Acts 1.1-15,35 (C. C. Torrey, *The Composition and Date of Acts*, 1916) or of Revelation (C. C. Torrey, *Documents of the Primitive Church*, 1941) could be demonstrated. This would show that much of the N.T. took form before Hellenistic influence had opportunity to distort the message. Such theories do call attention to the Aramaic-speaking background of the Gospel and warn against any view which asserts sweeping changes in the original message before the N.T. was written. On this subject see my *Origins of the Gospels*, 1938, and more recently M. Black, *An Aramaic Approach to the Gospels and Acts*, 1946.

parallels. It demands attention, however, that almost invariably they are only partial parallels. Moreover, in weighing such parallels two other questions must not be forgotten. In the first place, are there other, more frequent, and more vital parallels in the Old Testament and in Judaism, so that recourse to Gentile sources is not necessary to find the place of origin of such New Testament ideas? Such is often the case.[50] Secondly, can we explain the New Testament content by pointing to any or all of these parallels? Or do we have to find the creative and ruling center in the New Testament history itself, which alone can explain the nature and content of the New Testament gospel? Is the New Testament so disparate that the later part obscures and transforms the earlier message of Jesus and his first disciples, or does the entire New Testament portray a single organic movement centered in and moving out from Jesus, and thereby maintaining a basic unity and cohesiveness throughout?

VII

The answer can only be made by a series of propositions. In the first place, the alleged adaptation of the New Testament theology to the Gentile world can in any case be asserted only within strictly defined limits. As soon as we point out Christianity's instant and militant rejection of polytheism, it is clear that the New Testament has broken with a major portion of the Gentile world. We moderns speak with reverence of Athens and her art, but Athens was spiritually confused and impotent. Her public life was permeated with polytheism and her tolerant love of beauty sadly needed the backbone of a moral integrity derived from one great life-controlling faith. Athens and the other cities had their gods. The guilds had theirs. The govern-

---

[50] Useful in this field are H. L. Strack and P. Billerbeck, *Kommentar zum N.T. aus Talmud und Midrasch*, 4 vols., 1922-28, and the works of C. G. Montefiore and I. Abrahams.

ments had theirs, and in many cases even claimed that their sensual rulers were divine. In government, religion, business, amusement, labor, and social clubs the pagan world was built on the pattern of polytheism.[51]

The attitude of Apostolic Christianity to the polytheistic world was one of militant hostility.[52] Against the 'gods many and lords many' of that outside world (cf. Gal. 4.8), Paul and his fellow-Christians set the 'one God, the Father, and one Lord, Jesus Christ' (1 Cor. 8.6). They asked people to turn from idols (cf. Rom. 1.23) to serve the living and true God (1 Thess. 1.9). The Christian Church shared with Judaism the belief in angels both good and bad, but they were all created and redeemed by the Son (Col. 1.16,20). The stubborn evil hosts were defeated by Christ (Col. 2.15), and the obedient ones were 'ministering spirits' of God (Heb. 1.14). In neither case were they effective rivals of the Lord of Heaven and Earth. Christianity was a rejection of polytheism. To supporters of the first-century *status quo* these Christians 'have turned the world upside down' (Acts 17.6).

VIII

In the second place, the Hellenistic character of the later books of the New Testament has often been overstated. There

---

[51] On the exceedingly complex religious situation in the Hellenistic world, see Halliday, *op. cit.*; S. Angus, *The Religious Quests of the Graeco-Roman World*, 1929; G. H. C. Macgregor and A. C. Purdy, *Jew and Greek: Tutors unto Christ*, 1936. Too often, as in the last-named book, the theme of 'preparation' for Christianity obscures the *break* with the past which the Christian preachers required polytheists to make. Moreover, the extent to which every-day life was permeated with polytheistic rites and references is often overlooked. Even philosophers in many cases conformed to such practices; they 'interpreted' them, but they did not break with them.

[52] The most lenient treatment of polytheism and idolatry is that of Acts 17.22-31 (cf. 14.15 f.). Yet here, as always, a clean break with the polytheistic past is demanded.

is no thoroughly Greek or Hellenistic book in the New Testament. Most of these books are obviously alien to the general Hellenistic outlook. Moreover, in the case of those books which have been regarded as Hellenistic, the solid Jewish foundation is still the more obvious setting of the specifically Christian content which the writings contain.

The Epistle of James has been compared with the Hellenistic wisdom writings.[53] The unique feature of this book is that it has so little distinctively Christian content. Yet it has notable parallels with the Sermon on the Mount;[54] moreover, it recalls Judaism in its references to such topics as respect of persons, faith and works, the day of the Lord, and the prophets. It is not a truly Hellenistic document.

The Epistle to the Hebrews reminds us at times of Plato's doctrine of ideas, and of Philo's echo of Platonism, yet even this phase of the thought of the Epistle has some relation to the Old Testament,[55] and its solid substance is so thoroughly Jewish that it is only by a lame case of special pleading that one can speak of it as a Hellenistic product.

Second Peter has impressed scholars at times as illustrating the trend to Hellenistic life (cf. 1.5-7). However, as quotations and allusions show, the background of this writing is dominantly Old Testament and Jewish. Moreover, the moral laxity which this Epistle considers the immediate danger to the very life of the Christian Church finds its excuse in the Hellenistic dualism of matter and spirit, a dualism which Judaism, in keeping

[53] Upon examination, such comparisons relate James to Jewish wisdom writings, some of which were composed in Greek. It is clear that Hellenistic Judaism borrowed elements from the surrounding world, but in its own view and in the judgment of Gentiles, it was a part of Judaism and essentially separate from its Gentile environment. Its apologetics and proselytism were marks of conscious aloofness from general Gentile life and culture.

[54] See J. B. Mayor, *The Epistle of St. James*, 1897, pp. lxxxiv f. Mayor deals in detail with the parallels in the O.T., the N.T., and the Hellenistic writings.

[55] Platonic idea and O.T. reference appear combined in Heb. 8.5.

with the Old Testament, instinctively rejected, and which Christianity in the New Testament almost completely avoided.[56]

The one book, therefore, which may with any plausibility be claimed to embody the Hellenization of the Gospel is the Gospel of John. There are indeed features of the Fourth Gospel which show the desire to reach the Gentile world. This is not surprising or evil; it is necessary and desirable. But there are facts to take into account on the other side. The Gospel itself reminds the reader that ' salvation is of the Jews ' (4.22). The story it tells does not move out of Jewish circles except in the symbolic scene when the ' Greeks ' ask to ' see Jesus ' (12.20 ff.), and even here no actual meeting is reported; the essential content of the passage is that the Gentile mission is the right result of the full work of Christ. Moreover, Abrahams, a Jewish scholar, found that the discourses of the Gospel of John have a Jewish ring.[57] Burney, Torrey, and others have argued that the Gospel was first written in Aramaic.[58] In other words, the claim that the Fourth Gospel is Hellenistic is one-sided. It ignores the fact that this is a bridge type of document, which comes out of one atmosphere and reaches effectively into another.

An illustration of this breadth of outlook is the use of the Logos doctrine, whose role in the Gospel should not be overrated. Alleged parallels and sources have been found in both Jewish and Gentile circles.[59] This is precisely the characteristic of the Gospel which needs more attention than it usually receives. The author looks to a wider public and horizon than the Jewish world. But he has no intention of abandoning the

[56] The tendency to asceticism in 1 Cor. 7 is at least partly due to eschatological expectation. Paul's references to the ' flesh ' involve the will and are not expressive of metaphysical dualism.

[57] In *Cambridge Biblical Essays*, 1909, p. 181.

[58] See note 49.

[59] On the various backgrounds see Kittel's *Theologisches Wörterbuch zum N.T.*, Vol. IV, pp. 73-100. Cf. also W. F. Howard, *Christianity According to St. John*, 1946, Chap. 2.

Jewish heritage or of surrendering to the Gentile world. His God is the Jewish God. His Logos is the historical Jew Jesus, seen in his full nature and significance. His Scripture is the Old Testament. His message offers both kinship and challenge to Greek and Jewish thought alike, but the high degree of Jewish background and influence requires rigid limitation of the role of Hellenistic thought and religion even in this apparently most Hellenistic of the New Testament books.

IX

In the third place, the New Testament combination of God's sovereign transcendence and his gracious redemptive action finds no real parallel in the Gentile world. Transcendent gods there were; indeed, to hear the Epicureans tell the story, that was almost a complete description of the gods. But such gods were not sovereign; they were merely remote and indifferent. Nor were they active to initiate and effect redemption; they were not concerned about such things.

The Olympian gods were apparently superior to men.[60] Such polytheistic pantheons, however, were a poor form of either sovereignty or transcendence; they exhibited a continuous condition of civil war and intrigue and immoral affairs; they were animated by jealousy and formed a mutually self-limiting group. Least of all could their rule, though it might at times favor fortunate individuals, be described as one of redemptive grace. It was rather a quest for honor and favors, often to the point of cheap petulance.

The Stoics offered a more vital picture of the divine activity in the world. But this immanence was not properly grace; it was not redemptive in the New Testament sense; it was

[60] The worship of the Olympian deities and their Roman counterparts continued, although with a considerable tinge of sophistication or skepticism, and aided no doubt by the prompting of classical art and literature.

rather the potential capacity for self-salvation, limited by a conception of the order of nature as a fate or destiny.[61] There is here no such sovereignty as the Bible ascribes to the Lord God of all, and no such spiritual sense of transcendence as underlay the Biblical reverence and awe.

We may turn to Plato, who rises above the ancient pagan world in so many respects. But the text-books on philosophy deal gently with his dualism, and with some of his sex ideas.[62] The ancient world did not get from him that sense of the personal, free, sovereign, holy God, nor of the divine outreaching, costly, redemptive grace, which it found in the Bible. There are many points of agreement and many parallels. Yet one cannot find in Plato the full range and depth of the New Testament message of the God and Father of our Lord Jesus Christ. One might conceivably regard the Platonic idea as superior, but he cannot say that the two positions are identical. Least of all can it be said that the New Testament God, the Redeemer and Lord, the Father of Christ, is in any essential derived from Platonic thought.

x

In the fourth place, the distinctive New Testament combination of the sovereign transcendence and initiating grace works out in a view of God as *both* Creator and Redeemer which is not derived from nor matched by the thought of the Hellenistic world. The New Testament shares with the Old Testament

---

[61] Cf. C. N. Cochrane, *Christianity and Classical Culture*, 1944, p. 165.

[62] Cf. F. Thilly, *A History of Philosophy*, 1914, p. 69: 'The body is the prison-house of the soul, a fetter. . . . The release of the soul from the body and the contemplation of the beautiful world of ideas, that is the ultimate end of life.' Although A. E. Taylor, *Plato: The Man and His Work*, 1929, p. 277, denies that Book Five of the Republic calls for 'community of women,' the ideal of monogamous marriage is not there found. Cf. Mark 10.2-12 as a contrast.

and with Judaism the faith that the world which he created was good. All dualism between matter and spirit is decisively excluded by this view, and this marks a real difference between most Greek thought and the New Testament.[63]

Moreover, all emanation theories of man's origin are likewise excluded.[64] Man himself is the chief and final work of God's creative action. He is made in the image of God, but he is not a fragment of God. God's purpose in making man was gracious, and in spite of the sin of man the divine purpose persisted in acts of redemption for Israel, a working which came to its climax in Christ. This God is righteous, but his righteousness acts not only to thwart and judge evil but above all to save those who trust him. There is unity and consistency in this continuing action of the holy God to create and benefit man.

The New Testament works out this unity from the central figure, Jesus Christ. It finds the significance of what he did so great that his work cannot be confined to one time and place. It ends with a view of Christ as the Son and Logos who acts for God in the entire range of his gracious purpose, from the original creation to the central redemptive activity in history and on to the final new creation (1 Cor. 8.6; Col. 1.13 ff.; Heb. 1.1-4; John 1.1 ff.; Rev. 19.11 ff.).

In the expression of this faith the New Testament uses many

[63] Where matter is evil or is not a part of God's creation, the body may be regarded as a 'tomb,' as in much Greek thought; redemption then consists essentially of escape from the material, and a Docetic view of the body of Jesus becomes a necessity of Christian faith. Against this morally weak view the N.T. finds man's dilemma not in matter but in the will, hence the continual use of the imperative and the despair when the will is impotent (Rom 7.7 ff.). Moreover, 'the Word became flesh' (John 1.14); Docetism is unavoidable in dualistic thought and intolerable for Christian faith. Even the believer's body is 'a temple of the Holy Spirit' (1 Cor. 6.19).

[64] The purpose of an emanation theory is generally to explain how any part of the divinely pure spirit world got mired down in defiling matter. Redemption will consist of escape from matter. The preceding, of course, is not a complete presentation of emanation ideas.

ideas and terms which have either parallels or origin in the Hellenistic world. It had to do so in order to make its message intelligible. But our question is whether the view which the New Testament presents of God as the Creator *and* Redeemer is in essential aspects derived from Hellenistic sources, or whether it derives consistently and naturally from the actual career of Jesus. The interpretation of that career as God's central and decisive historical action goes back to Jesus and the earliest Jewish Christians (Mark 1.15; Acts 2.14-36; 1 Cor. 15.3 ff.). [65] It is stated in terms which derive largely from Judaism but are given a unique reference through Christ.

It is not possible to derive this essential New Testament conviction and faith from Hellenistic sources. This unified view of the divine action of creation and redemption through Christ grows out of the career and work of Christ and the realization of the Apostolic Church that in Christ God had dealt uniquely with them for their good (2 Cor. 5.19). It would be a radical error, a fatal error, to forget this central fact in a search for this or that respect in which the thought and life of the Apostolic Church was affected and shaped by ideas which were native to or chiefly characteristic of the Hellenistic world. That search is legitimate, but only when its secondary role has become clear.

XI

In the fifth place, the high Christology which marks the New Testament goes back too early, and is too widely prevalent in the New Testament, to allow the view that its origin roots essentially in the Hellenistic world. To be sure, the opposite view has been maintained. For example, Bousset argued that the view of Christ as Lord was a Hellenistic addition to the

[65] See Dodd, *op cit.*, on the use of the speeches of Acts.

original Gospel.[66]   Others have found in the mystery religions
the source of much of the Pauline Gospel;[67] they have then cut
out of the Gospels the chain of passages which point to the
Pauline views; they have likewise discounted all statements of
the early part of Acts which agree with the Pauline note.

The predominant Jewish atmosphere in the New Testament,
however, makes it difficult to date the rise of such central themes
as the Lordship of Christ, and his death and resurrection for
man's benefit, so late that Jewish setting and influence are excluded.   The Apostolic Church had too strong a proportion of
Jews, and it had too predominantly a Jewish Christian leadership, to leave open the possibility of a directly and purely Gentile
origin of essential features of the New Testament faith.

The only form in which any significant Hellenistic influence
could have been exercised so early was by way of Hellenistic
Judaism.[68]   Since the New Testament was written in Greek, or
at least was in large part written in Greek, such a shaping of
the Gospel among Jewish disciples of Hellenistic culture is
theoretically possible.   Since Jesus spoke Aramaic in teaching,
at least as a prevailing practice, and the Gospel almost immediately spread into the Greek-speaking circle of Judaism and thus
into the Gentile world, it may be asked whether the message
concerning God underwent a radical change in the course of
this transfer and expansion.

Such a view can be supported only by a radical rejection of
the New Testament.   This is not a final argument, since it is the
point under consideration.   But the quantity of evidence should
be made clear.   Take the Lord concept as an example.   We are
not discussing some minor point which occurs but occasionally.
On the contrary, Jesus is called Lord in practically every book

[66] *Kyrios Christos*, third ed., 1926, p. 101. Bousset holds that the Hellenistic Christians used the O.T. references to the 'Lord' only after they
had derived their central conception elsewhere.
[67] Cf. E. W. Parsons, *The Religion of the New Testament*, 1939, p. 99,
on the origin of Paul's sacramental views.
[68] Bousset is of this view.

which the New Testament contains.[69] The term is used of him in reference to his lifetime, and in the report of the preaching of the earliest Church when only Jews were being approached. If the term is a later insertion into the stream of Christian thought and usage, that fact is quite concealed. The New Testament unitedly witnesses to the contrary; in it the term is used of Jesus by Jesus himself and by his earliest preachers in the Apostolic Age and by all those who write of him.

A second relevant observation is that Paul gives the strongest possible evidence for concluding that the term was not strange to Aramaic-speaking Christians in the earliest days of the Church. He indirectly testifies that the term Lord was used by such Aramaic-speaking Christians; this he does when he uses the Aramaic term Maranatha (1 Cor. 16.22), which means ' Our Lord, Come ! '[70] Moreover, although he himself is a Greek-speaking Christian in almost all of his evangelistic work in Acts, he so uses the term here as to show that it means much to him in its Aramaic form. He is not reporting that others use this term, but is using it himself as an earnest prayer for the coming of the Lord. His Greek word *Kyrios*, therefore, was a translation and equivalent of the Aramaic word *Mar*, which was so widely used of Christ and so meaningful to him that in a moment of deepest prayer it came to fervent expression. The idea that the Aramaic-speaking Church was in radical disagreement with the Greek-speaking Church in its Christology receives a severe jolt from this prayer usage of Paul.

But there is more to say. The more we study the letters of Paul, the more we realize that he takes it for granted at all times that he and the other Apostolic leaders are in essential

---

[69] The title is lacking only in the Johannine Epistles; this omission is not significant in view of John 20.28, which represents the faith of the Johannine circle. Moreover, 2 John 3 contains the title in some manuscripts.

[70] The translation as an imperative rather than as an indicative is rightly favored by O. Cullmann, *Christ and Time*, Eng. tr., 1950, p. 74. It is evident that the title *Mar* is used here of a person who is regarded with reverence and faith.

accord in their faith in Jesus and their thought concerning him (cf. Gal. 2.6; I Cor. 15.11). As to the Law he may argue. But he gives no hint, nor does any other New Testament writer,[71] of a breach between himself and his fellow-Apostles in essential Christology. I personally have no doubt that in content and conceptual framework the commonly used terms Christ, Son of God, and Lord varied from time to time and from Jewish to Gentile setting. But in every case they expressed the conviction that Jesus played a unique role, was unique in person and character, and stood in a unique relation to God.

The leaders of the Church were deeply convinced that they held the same faith. Paul explicity asserts that this was the case. When we remember that, according to his own statement (I Cor. 11.23; 15.3), he had 'received' the tradition which he passed on to the Corinthians, and that his conversion must be dated not later than the middle thirties,[72] his basic agreement with the Jerusalem Apostles becomes a fact of the greatest significance for historical study. It is a fact that has too often been ignored or evaded. It takes the essential Christology of the Church back into the days when only Jewish Christian Christology was possible, when Gentile influence was hardly practical, and when the companions of Jesus, the eye-witnesses of his ministry, were prominent in the Church.[73] They agreed with Paul in what he preached. This is the fact which no difference in detail can obscure. Jesus Christ was central and

[71] The idea that the Synoptic Gospels present a pre-Pauline and non-Christological picture of Jesus is absurd. Every gospel writer or writer of a gospel source was a believer in Jesus as Lord and Christ. The Gospels are post-Pauline and are not anti-Pauline (not even Matt., except possibly in minor points). See E. F. Scott, *The Purpose of the Gospels*, 1949.
[72] Exact chronology is unattainable. It is possible that his conversion occurred early in the thirties, assuming A.D. 30 as probable date for the crucifixion, and it is extremely improbable that it took place later than A.D. 36. In any event, the point stated above is valid.
[73] On the steadying role of eye-witness of Jesus' ministry, see V. Taylor, *The Formation of the Gospel Tradition*, 1933, pp. 41-43.

determinative in the faith of all these leaders; he was Lord and
Son of God as well as Christ.

Once this fact is recognized, there is no longer any need or
room for the view that the speeches of Acts represent only
Pauline and post-Pauline ideas, or that the Gospels must under-
go numerous excisions in order to remove the Paulinism which
has infected them. No, this so-called 'Paulinism,' as Martin
Werner[74] noted in regard to Mark, turns out to be an essential
part of the common message. Paul in his preaching had his
own elaborations and emphases, but his basic message was not
his own original creation; it was the apostolic message, which
appeared much too early to allow us to accept any theory that
the Gospel derived its essential content from Hellenistic thought,
even through the medium of Hellenistic Judaism. If there was
intrusion or perversion, it came almost instantly, in one immediate and radical transformation.

C. C. Torrey sensed this.[75] It has not always been noticed
that he proposed a clear explanation of the origin of historic
Christianity. So much attention has been paid to his theory of
the Aramaic originals of the Gospels that this larger theory has
often escaped attention. His view is that Judaism, building
upon the Old Testament and indeed merely reproducing the
Old Testament picture found in Second Isaiah, had already
constructed a complete outline of what the Messiah would be
and do. Jesus did not appear to fulfil that expectation, and did
not suspect that he and his work were to be connected with
that expectation which 'everyone,' to use Torrey's own word,
held in the first century. But as soon as Jesus had been put to
death and his followers had rallied, they had available this ready-
made and complete picture, which they simply applied to Jesus.
Why they rallied and why they connected this picture with Jesus,
if he did not do so and had not seemed to fulfil the expectation,
I will not attempt to explain, and I do not think anyone can

[74] *Der Einfluss paulinischer Theologie im Markusevangelium*, 1923.
[75] *Our Translated Gospels*, 1936. See the Introduction, pp. xv-xlix.

explain. But Torrey does not see that from the first days of the Apostolic Church an explicit and high Christology was an integral part of its message, and that this Christology was basically no Hellenistic product, but had its chief ties with the Old Testament and found expression in the earliest Apostolic Preaching.

Torrey's view of Gospel origins I reject. The Aramaic origin of the Gospels has not been proved, and I do not expect it to be proved. That Jesus spoke Aramaic, and that our tradition came in part through an Aramaic-speaking Church in the earliest days, is the truth in the theory. But with that question we are not now concerned. We want to know where the Christology of the Apostolic Church took its rise. The answer should not be in doubt. The Resurrection stands at the opening of the Apostolic Age to shape and condition all faith and thought. The career of Jesus Christ—his ministry, death, and Resurrection—this is what the Church has always given as the basis of its Christology. From this original content derived the doctrine of God as the God and Father of our risen Lord Jesus Christ.

The crucial point is therefore the Resurrection. Deny that, and then one may well need the influence of some other factor to explain the Christology and theology of the Apostles and New Testament writers.[76] But given the truth of that, the Christology of the Apostolic Age becomes consistent and natural. This risen Jesus was proclaimed from the first as 'Lord and Christ' (Acts 2.36); there was no reason at all for the disciples to question that he was the unique Son of God. Whether the Jewish disciples thought in the precise metaphysical patterns which later Greek Christians and creed writers used is open to question. I personally think it but natural to assume that early Christian thinking developed, and that Oriental and Greek ideas influenced Christianity as it spread in the Gentile world. But this affects secondary matters. The

[76] A. M. Ramsey, *The Resurrection of Christ*, 1946, points out the need for a view of the resurrection which will 'account for the Gospel which the Apostles preached and by which the first Christians lived' (p. 57).

real issue lies deeper: Are we to explain the rise of Christianity in its classical form by the distorting influence of other religious ideas and cults, or by the more clearly seen significance of the central affirmations in its tradition? To be specific, is the central place and redemptive meaning given to the Cross and Resurrection a borrowing from the nature cults, the mystery religions,[77] or is it a reflection of the fact that among Jews, in Palestine, in circles which were at least prevailingly Aramaic-speaking, faith in the Resurrection arose and became the interpreting basis of the view that the Cross was important in God's working and that Jesus' entire ministry was the work of the Christ and Son of God?

This may be resolved into two questions: First, was it in fact the Resurrection faith which gave the impetus to the rise of the Apostolic Church and the affirmation of a high Christology? To this question one must answer yes. One may claim that the disciples were deluded, but they undeniably did build upon the Resurrection. They interpreted the entire career, and went on in a very few years to interpret the entire work of God the Father, in the light of this unique fact. The second question is the only one concerning which there can be dispute: Did God raise Jesus from the dead? Did Jesus come back to restored personal relations with his disciples and resume the leadership of his group, first through such occasional contacts with the leaders, and then, as the Lord of his people, through the Holy Spirit?

What historical study does is to lead us back to this alternative: Either the disciples were radically mistaken and deluded, or Christ was risen and Christianity given a basis which cannot be explained by borrowing or dependence upon either Jewish or Gentile sources. The Christian message about Christ the Risen Lord and God as his Father is either history's most influential mistake, a mistake made by Aramaic-speaking Jews, or it is a distinctive and valid message unique in content and in relevance for faith.

[77] See S. Angus, *The Mystery Religions and Christianity*, 1925.

CHAPTER TWO

'THE FULLNESS OF TIME'

THE comparison of the New Testament understanding of history with views current in first-century Jewish and Hellenistic circles seems at first sight an easy task. With Judaism the new Christian movement shared an emphasis on history which grew out of Israel's faith and religious observances; common ground is clearly present. The Greeks are generally recognized to have been the creators of history as a scientific study,[1] a fact which might suggest to the unwary that the New Testament, written in Greek and intended for use in the Greek-speaking world, would fit into the Greek outlook.

The situation is not so simple, however, and for three reasons. Faith in Christ led the Christians to give the Old Testament story a new conclusion and interpretation, which Judaism refused to accept. Christian faith in the working of God in history also resulted in a view markedly different from that which prevailed in the Greek world. Moreover, the modern Church often misunderstands its relation to the Old Testament and Israel, and often inclines to prefer the Greek attitude to the New Testament view; as a result our discussion of the problem of history encounters unusual difficulties. It is necessary therefore to state fully the New Testament understanding of history, in order to make clear its contrast with non-Christian views.

The statement that Christianity is a historical religion is indeed true, but the specific meaning of the adjective is not immediately clear. To speak of Christianity as a historical faith

[1] See J. W. Thompson, *A History of Historical Writing*, 1942, Vol. I, Chap. 2, 'Ancient Greek Historiography,' and his quotation on p. 21 from U.v. Wilamowitz-Moellendorf, *Greek Historical Writing and Apollo*, Eng. tr., 1908, pp. 5 f.: 'All our historical writing rests on foundations laid by the Greeks.'

does not mean merely that it has had a long history, which the modern believer or student must understand. Nor does it imply only that at the point of origin of this faith we find a known founder, and that we can name the most important of his first followers.

Least of all does the description mean that we can fully understand Christianity by such research and method as is commonly used to understand and write the history of any other people or movement. To be sure, this latter mistake has often been made in recent times. The ideal method, it has been supposed, is to free oneself from all personal attitudes and preferences, regard the emerging faith in a neutral and purely 'objective' way, and so understand it as it really was.[2] It has been thought that to let personal faith enter into the consideration would be to warp the facts and distort the resulting picture; to avoid this mistake, it has been held, the student must take a rigidly objective position, seek for the actual facts and situation, and report what he finds.

Every New Testament reporter would rise in protest against this procedure, for it is diametrically opposed to the one which they exemplify. The modern scholar may decide that these ancient authors were quite mistaken, but he cannot deny that they all do their work as professed partisans; they are vigorous witnesses. They were as concerned to give the reader 'assured results' as was Thucydides,[3] but would have rejected the idea that any one should be neutral concerning the history of which

[2] Cf. Thucydides' preface to his *History of the Peloponnesian War*, in which he states that his aim is not to satisfy romantic interest but to tell 'exactly how things happened in the past.' The meaning of 'objective' in modern historical study deserves attention; it involves a renunciation of religious presuppositions, and a limitation of study to the outwardly observable data of nature and of personal and group life. This conception has a basis in Thucydides' attitude.

[3] Cf. the purpose of Thucydides (note 2) with the expressed intent of Luke: 'that thou mightest know the certainty" (Luke 1.4). Both aim to tell the significant truth in correct perspective, but the perspective differs.

they tell. In their mind, no one has intellectual or moral justification for remaining detached from the message and movement which they report.

If, then, we say that they tell a history, and that for them the Christian faith is a historical religion, we must seek first of all to understand the particular sense in which this statement is true. What does the New Testament itself mean when it presents Christianity as a historical religion?

1. It must first be noted that this New Testament history is amazingly selective. Its Old Testament basis follows the story of a small people. In the New Testament it concentrates upon one central figure and the relatively few individuals who are closely connected with him. These leading individuals did not possess high social standing or even general esteem. The founder had been condemned as a criminal or rebel, and the early Church leaders repeatedly incurred public displeasure. Numerically the Apostolic Church was never significant. In social, cultural, political, and economic position both the chief characters and the general membership of the Christian group were so weak that its later expansion appears to offer a curious puzzle.[4] The movement took its rise in a small border province whose people were subjects of Rome.

Yet the Gospel asserts that in the story of this founder, these Apostles, this small and apparently discredited movement in this insignificant area, is contained the hope of the world as well as of each individual. The message declares that this outwardly unimpressive and apparently pitiful history is the most important series of happenings in the entire sweep of world events. Whatever universalism the Gospel contains is coupled

---

[4] While 1 Cor. 1.26-29 describes only one local church group, the unpretentious Nazareth origin of Jesus, the obscure origin of the Twelve, the poverty in the Jerusalem Church and its repeated need of outside help (Acts 4.34 ff.; 11.29; Gal. 2.10), and the evidence that numerous slaves were in the Church (Acts 12.13?; Col. 3.22-4.1; Phm.) are in accord with Paul's description. Neither the Jewish nor the Gentile Christians would have been regarded as the 'cream' of society in that period.

with this peculiar particularism, which constitutes an essential feature of the story.

2. It must next be observed that the history the New Testament tells is an *interpreted history*. This will no longer seem so strange and objectionable as might have been the case a generation or two ago. In our day scholars increasingly recognize that there is no such thing as the uninterpreted presentation or past events. The process of selecting, interrelating, and understanding what took place in the past involves the scholar in an interpretative procedure.[5] Whether he knows it or not, he must assume certain principles and pass crucial judgments. All history is thus a combination of past event and discerning interpretation.

This method characterizes the skeptic and professed neutral as much as it does the convinced believer. One delusion which it is high time to discard is the idea that while dedicated adherents of a religious faith are biased, persons who are without such faith or who detach themselves from their faith are thereby in a position to be balanced, competent, and free from distortion. This claim has always been a baseless presumption. Every person has his interpreting standpoint. The question is, Whose position is more nearly correct?

To take a quite obvious example, Saul knew before his conversion that Jesus had been 'crucified under Pontius Pilate.' At that time the fact was to him proof positive that Jesus was an impostor who deserved the cruel execution which openly discredited him.[6] After Saul was converted, however, the same

[5] J. T. Shotwell, *The History of History*, Vol. I, 1939, p. 250, points out that the great Greek historians were 'interpreters of processes or trends.' Cf. C. H. Dodd, *History and the Gospels*, 1938, pp. 27 f.: 'The record brings out the meaning of events. . . . The feelings and judgments of the human mind enter into the process. . . . A series of events is most truly apprehended and recorded when it is apprehended in some measure from within the series and not from an entirely detached standpoint.'

[6] Gal. 3.13, with its quotation of Deut. 21.23, may well have as background Paul's pre-Christian condemnation of Jesus on the basis of the Deuteronomy passage.

fact, the crucifixion, took on a radically different aspect; it now became a crowning demonstration of the spirit and purpose of Christ; it revealed the grace of God himself (2 Cor. 5.14-21; Rom. 5.8). In both periods he interpreted the story.

If it be replied that in both cases Paul was a partisan, and so in neither case could be a competent witness, two things may be said. In the first place, it is clear from this example—and the same thing can be illustrated by the amazing contrast between the Christian Gospels and the hostile and hopelessly garbled Jewish tradition about Jesus which survives in rabbinical sources[7]—that hate is by no means a better aid to interpretation than are faith and love. Saul the persecutor is not to be preferred to Paul the Apostle as an interpreter of Jesus Christ.

The second thing to say is that the supposedly neutral witnesses concerning Jesus are nowhere to be found. The inevitability of interpretation is equally clear when we consider the reaction of Pilate or Tacitus. Pilate, a man of experience and in a position to seek the facts, did not understand Jesus nor do him justice, but he did form an estimate of him; he regarded the prisoner as perhaps deluded and in any case unimportant.[8] Tacitus was writing serious history, but his scornful, fleeting reference to Jesus and the Christians[9] was an interpretation, and who can fairly say that it was better than that of Paul or Luke?

Such ancient 'neutrals' hardly rival the New Testament reporters as guides to the understanding of Jesus. Nor are they neutral. In the long run, they could not be, for interpretation is involved in all life and reporting, and particularly in dealing with the New Testament message, which insists upon decision

[7] See R. T. Herford, *Christianity in Talmud and Midrash*, 1903; J. Klausner, *Jesus of Nazareth*, Eng. tr., 1925, pp. 18-54.
[8] The decision concerning execution or release was in Pilate's hands. He was clear that Jesus did not deserve condemnation as a rebel, but he also saw that Jesus had no political support and was a 'visionary idealist' whom political expediency might safely sacrifice.   [9] *Annals*, XV.44.

and participation. The New Testament story couples interpretation and appeal with its report of what happened; it claims that the interpretation is an integral part of the story and inevitably involves an urgent appeal to the hearer. Any other thorough presentation of this story will likewise be an interpretation.

3. A third observation simply makes explicit what we implied when we said that the New Testament is interpreted history. All of this particular story is seen through the eyes of faith; it is given an added dimension. Only so does the story escape condemnation as petty and insignificant. There is more here than meets the eye of outward vision. We said above that in the New Testament the happening is interpreted; here we emphasize that it is interpreted not merely by psychological sensitiveness or social imagination, but chiefly by religious faith, which declares that in these events it has been confronted by a divine claim which calls for something far deeper than an intellectual or sympathetic response. Faith introduces a dimension which goes beyond the psychological and social interpretation of occurrence.

4. In the fourth place, the eye of faith, which sees that the happenings reported possess an added dimension, groups together things which the objective historian sharply separates. We encounter in the New Testament not only narratives of happenings which any alert person could have observed, but also such stories as those concerning the entry of the Son of God into human life, his resurrection from the dead, and the descent of the Holy Spirit. These things are stated as essential facts, and they are told with the same calm assurance which marks the reports that Jesus was friendly to outcasts and that he taught in parables. The story moves in an atmosphere which neither feels nor tolerates a sharp dividing line between the two groups of material.[10]

[10] See O. Cullmann, *Christ and Time*, Eng. tr., 1950, on ' The Connection Between History and Prophecy (History and Myth),' pp. 94 ff.

The historian usually sets aside as myth or legend the one type of tradition, and turns to the other data, which anyone may verify, for the historical material which he may use in writing of Jesus. The New Testament has no such 'middle wall of partition.' Why? From the viewpoint of the added dimension which we have noted, both types of tradition are fully credible and each type is thoroughly consistent with the other. They are bound together by the fact that faith sees an added dimension even in outwardly verifiable events. We may find reasons to call in question items of both kinds of tradition, and in certain respects we may justify the division of the tradition into two parts, but we cannot find in the New Testament any sense that there are two kinds. There is simply the witness to Jesus Christ presented through the eyes of faith.

5. The added dimension which faith discerns identifies God as the chief actor. Such is the fifth and final observation in our description of the New Testament understanding of history. This ancient account intends to tell what God has done. It sees the unity of history in the continuing and purposeful working of God in successive stages. When it presents Christianity as a historical religion it means that God himself has acted in history in such a way as to call for a response of faith (2 Cor. 5.18-20).

This is the scandal which the so-called objective historian finds in the New Testament. These writings take a position which in his work he must reject at the outset and exclude from every stage of his study. He is committed to write a history by leaving out of account the one fact which alone made the story significant to the New Testament writers. His account leaves out the initiative and working of God, who in the New Testament is the creative, dominating, all-pervasive factor.[11]

The 'objective' historian may reply that he fully recognizes that these writers spoke concerning God. They held, however,

[11] See my essay on 'The Central Problem Concerning Christian Origins,' in *The Study of the Bible Today and Tomorrow*, edited by H. R. Willoughby, 1947, pp. 329-44.

that their human ideas of God were not of primary importance; to deal with their ideas and stop there would be either an evasion or a rejection. They had only one interest, which was to say that God had acted and that every hearer and reader of the Gospel was confronted not by man's ideas but by God's own action and claim. Their story had one point, namely, that in what human actors did it was really God who was at work; indeed, in the central Figure of the story God was present or, better, active in a unique and commanding way. Their history, therefore, was not intended primarily as a story about men or their ideas or social relations; it was a message about the working of God. He works in history; he works with men; they must make their choice before him and in the light of what he has done and requires; he is working to a goal; man's place and privilege is in the framework of that divine action.

So it is correct to speak of this new faith as a historical religion. But we see now that for the New Testament history is a God-centered concept; in essence it is an account of what God has done, is doing, and will do. God has revealed himself in specific acts which he has done through special individuals and a particular group.[12] History, that is, a quite particular history, is the medium of the revelation of God. In this point of view the New Testament is solidly united with the Old Testament and so is closely akin to Judaism, but it is quite out of keeping with the dominant spirit of Hellenistic thought, in which the real advance of divine action and its eschatological goal play no such role.[13]

[12] In Christian theology that is faithful to its Biblical basis attention to redemptive history and an organization which takes account of God's historical action may be expected. Much recent 'theology' has been apologetics and philosophy of religion, and has lacked a proper historical basis.

[13] The lack of a great expectation, a real eschatology growing out of the divine action, is typical of Greek historiography, as K. Löwith notes in Meaning in History, 1949, pp. 5 ff. Without such an expectation, both mythology and history had essentially a backward reference; the future would in general repeat the past. Cf. F. H. Brabant, Time and Eternity in Christian Thought, 1937, p. 32: 'The Greeks . . . did not seem able to grasp the idea of a purpose behind history.'

II

The fact that God has revealed himself in a definite thread of history and that the Gospel is therefore a story carries with it the essential point that time is real to the New Testament mind. Time has been a problem to numerous thinkers in both ancient and modern days. Many a restless mind has made a persistent struggle to escape from this time framework of existence. In his thinking man has repeatedly sought to find an exit into timeless, placid eternity.[14] That, men keep thinking, is where God is. That is where the solution of our problems of life and thought will be found. On this view, a primal curse rests upon the particularity of historical events; they at best can give us only broken fragments of the eternal truth, and they inevitably obscure the greater truths. What we need therefore is to grasp truth, especially the Gospel, in forms which are not time-cramped.

A recent example of this attitude is Rudolf Bultmann's attempt to 'demythologize' the Gospel.[15] He seeks a substitute for the New Testament method of presenting saving truth in the form of a particular history. He sees this framework as a dispensable myth which now obscures the essential Gospel. But his dissatisfaction with the Gospel story, in which a specific series of events is interpreted as the decisive action of God in time, is not peculiar to him or to a small group. It has been widely felt.

[14] As Brabant, *op. cit.*, p. 21, notes, eternity for Plato means 'changelessness and order.'

[15] His essay in *Kerygma und Mytho*, edited by H. W. Bartsch, 1948, pp. 15-53, 'Neues Testament und Mythologie,' is an earnest attempt to state the Gospel in a form which will preserve its content and also appeal to the modern man. The framework for restatement is the existentialist philosophy. Other essays in the same volume charge Bultmann with surrendering the true historical character of the Gospel. He denies this in his rejoinders, but his essay seeks to discard the framework of redemptive history.

In contrast with all such disparagement or discarding of the time framework of the Gospel message, Oscar Cullmann, in his book on *Christ and Time*, has convincingly maintained that this framework is of the essence of the message. The New Testament, and indeed the entire Bible, does not speak of the mere existence of God, or of his static qualities or attributes. We know God in his acts;[16] we know him as he works in time; we know him as he manifests his purpose in a series of significant deeds; faith grasps the meaning of his successive actions, and bears witness to his character and claim by presenting the story of what he has done and is doing and will do. The only God the Bible knows is this God who acts. He makes himself known not in the isolated, timeless, mystical experience of the unrelated individual, but rather in the course of history and in individuals who are tied into that history.

The time framework is inseparable from the Gospel offer and promise. What we know of God prior to creation has to do with his intent; it is a time of preparation for creation and redemption. What we expect after this age ends is the sequel of the working of God in time, and so is conceived in time terms. The New Testament never escapes this time-determined form; it finds and proclaims God in his works in time. Its terms for eternity are terms which speak of an endless series of periods of time.[17]

In this connection it is interesting that when modern New Testament scholars try to express the New Testament content in terms of the timeless eternal rather than in terms of sequen-

---

[16] It is this redemptive action of God which Melanchthon had in mind when he said that 'this is to know Christ, to know his benefits.'

[17] Perhaps the most striking evidence for this is the use of the *plural* expressions 'into the ages' or 'into the ages of the ages.' The plural inescapably directs attention to a series of periods which follow one another in a time sequence. See Cullman, *op. cit.*, Part I, Chap. I, on 'The New Testament Terminology for Time.' It may be added that Rev. 10.6, which the A.V translates: 'that there should be time no longer,' really means that the end is to follow without further 'delay'; cf. E. J. Goodspeed, *Problems of N.T. Translation*, 1945, pp. 200 f.

tial time, they are driven to the use of terms which really have meaning only when time is taken seriously.[18] They use time terms; they are forced to use time terms; apart from these terms they give no positive or conceivable content to the eternity which they mention.

This, however, is not the main point which for me follows from Cullman's significant book. The central point is rather that if the Bible is at all dependable, the time process has meaning for God himself. He carries out his work by successive stages. He forms his plans in advance and executes them in the fullness of time.

It has often been asserted that God is separate from time and that all times are equally present to God. But this is *not* what the Bible says. It speaks with unshaken assurance of the action of God as constituting a real series of workings, one of which follows the preceding one in such a way that the sequence has meaning.[19]

The modern effort to rescue God from the supposed disgrace of involvement in time is thus a fretting which the Bible does not share. It is part of an attempt to make a Greek God who is free from any time quality, a so-to-speak 'docetic' God who is not really present and active in particular events, a God who is in general quite remote. But this is not the God of Abraham, Isaac, and Jacob, the God of Moses and the prophets, the God of the inbreaking Kingdom, the God whose Son, born into human life at a particular time, 'increased in wisdom and stature and in favor with God and man' (Luke 2.52), 'learned

[18] C. H. Dodd asserts that 'there is no before and after in the eternal order' and that '"The Day of the Son of Man" stands for the timeless fact' (*Parables of the Kingdom*, 1936, p. 108). To defend this position he has to maintain that the future tenses in Jesus' teaching 'are only an accommodation of language,' a statement that contradicts the obvious time reference of what Jesus said.

[19] 2 Pet. 3.8 says in effect that we cannot grasp God's time schedule, but it does not say that time has no meaning for him. The context of the verse clearly implies the opposite; God has acted and he will act.

obedience by the things which he suffered,' and was thus 'made perfect' (Heb. 5.8 f.) and competent to do at a particular point in time a decisive act for the everlasting benefit of God's people.[20]

No, this Biblical God, who works out his purpose in time, is not the God of the Greek philosophers, to whom time is rather a limitation or a problem,[21] nor of the Greek type of religion, nor of that bewildering variety of Gentile cults which have their roots in the nature cults with their meaningless cycle of the seasons.[22] It is the Old Testament God, now better known by reason of his further and decisive action in history and time.

III

The Gospel, then, is a story of a series of events in which God acts to carry forward his purpose to fulfilment. But the relation of the earthly career of Jesus Christ to the other stages of God's work requires careful statement.

We have seen in Chapter One that the entire New Testament regards Jesus as the central figure. The New Testament writers tell of him as not merely noble in life and masterly in teaching, but also redeeming in death and above all triumphant in resurrection. The Resurrection gives the vantage point from which the Cross is understood in its constructive significance and the ministry too is related to the plan and work of God. Even before the death and Resurrection, the message of the Kingdom and the claim of Jesus to act for God placed him in the center

[20] In the light of the Cross and its role in New Testament teaching the idea that God is remote from particular historical events and quite impassive is incongruous.

[21] Cf. R. Niebuhr, *Faith and History*, 1949, pp. 38 f.

[22] Most of the mystery religions were refined developments from earlier fertility cults, and they never fully escaped the framework of the annual seasons, which was their original form. See S. Angus, *The Mystery Religions and Christianity*, 1925, pp. 247 f.

of the course of divine action. After the Resurrection, however, his uniqueness, authority, and significance for God's redemptive work were still clearer, and his death took its place in a drama where it could not be a negative item but necessarily played a positive part in the full work of God through Christ. It called for a positive interpretation, which it received so early that when Paul was converted in the early or middle thirties of the first century,[23] he was told that 'Christ died for our sins according to the Scriptures' (1 Cor. 15.3). The ministry and death of Christ formed part of the divine action of God in Jesus, and they received their interpretation in the light of the foundation fact of all Christian preaching and thinking, namely, that God raised him from the dead and gave him the name and role of Lord.

At a chosen point in time (cf. Gal. 4.4) God did this unique act through a particular person for the benefit and help of all who thereafter put their lives in touch with his by faith. Everyone who hears the message should believe. All who believe know him as the living Lord (cf. Acts 2.36; 1 Cor. 12.3; John 20.28 f.). Of his Church he is the Lord and Head (Col. 1.18; Eph. 1.22). The time which follows until the final consummation is the time in which this Gospel is preached and men are called to believe in him and serve him. All time from the ministry of Christ is thus vitally related to his career and to him.

What is not so clear is how all preceding time is related to the central figure. Concerning the fact that in some way earlier times are so related there can be no doubt. Jesus preaches that 'the time is fulfilled' (Mark 1.15). He sees in what God is doing and about to do through him the fulfilment of the Old Testament anticipation and the Israelite hope. The Apostles from the first preached that in Christ this fulfilment has occurred. The citation of Scripture by the Gospel writers, the reference in the speeches of Acts to the progress of God's redemptive plan through the Old Testament period and on down

[23] On this date see note 72 in Chapter One.

to Christ the fulfilment,[24] and the similar statements and Scriptural quotations in the Epistles, all join in supporting the same viewpoint which Jesus' own life and teaching had expressed. The purpose of God with Israel came to its climax and realization in the work he did through Christ.

This does not mean that the New Testament narrative is merely an appendix or extension of the Old Testament story, and that in interpreting and relating the two, the dominant role should be assigned to the Old Testament. In the Christian message the significance of the Old Testament portion of the story is seen in the light of the climactic central action of God in Christ. The claim of the Gospel is that the Old Testament is not rightly or fully understood until it is seen in the light of the work of God in Christ (2 Cor. 3.14-16); the significance of the pre-Christian events is not really clear until their unity with the decisive central action is discerned.

The center of the divine action, then, is in the New Testament history. The focal point and interpreting center is Jesus Christ. This says much more than that he is the most important or pivotal figure of all history. That is certainly intended, but more is in mind. Not merely in man's view, but above all in God's own intent and action, Christ is central and decisive. Moreover, the true and full understanding of all stages and aspects of God's total work for men in history is to be gained by starting with Jesus Christ and relating everything to him.

Yet there is evidence that the study of the Old Testament and of the religious life of Israel, even among professing Christian

[24] On the substantial trustworthiness of these speeches see C. H. Dodd, *The Apostolic Preaching and its Developments*, 1937. The theological significance of the speeches should be noted. They are not included merely for literary variety or dramatic effect. They tell the story of God's redemptive action; they present the Gospel as a history. Exceptional are chaps. 14.15-17; 17.22-31. The usual speech pattern in Acts tells a story and refers to the history of Israel. Indeed, the Gospels, and especially Luke-Acts, are literary forms of a new kind; they have partial parallels or predecessors, but the embodiment of the Gospel in a history had and still has no full parallel.

scholars, may proceed without taking seriously this prominent feature of the New Testament content. An example is *The Religious Pilgrimage of Israel*, written by I. G. Matthews after a lifetime spent as a professor of Old Testament in a Christian seminary. How does this book relate the Old Testament story to Christ? The answer, briefly, is that it does not do so at all. Jesus is mentioned only once, in a prepositional phrase. The Christian movement finds mention in one paragraph only,[25] where the discussion does not deal with the Founder or the earliest days of the Church, but rather with the fall of Jerusalem and the final separation of the disciples of Jesus from official Judaism. That separation is regarded as quite legitimate. Not one word suggests that the pilgrimage of Israel was to Christ, or that Jesus, his Apostles, and the New Testament writers presented the Gospel as the urgent offer and inescapable challenge of God to Israel. On the contrary, in this book the pilgrimage of Israel is from the Old Testament through the Pharisees and rabbis to Talmudic Judaism and so on into mediaeval and modern Jewish life.

The author could doubtless say that he was describing the actual course of affairs, since in fact Judaism did continue on in the rabbinical and talmudic form. Such a view is intelligible, especially if made by a Jew or a professed neutral. What is inconceivable is that a Christian scholar could write the history of Judaism in the first century without explicit mention of the claim of Jesus and the Church and without making it clear that Judaism rejected a message which claimed to be the divinely effected fulfilment of the entire preceding history of God's dealings with his chosen people.

If the question involved the modern formulation of the Gospel, we could well grant that there are aspects which are due to the long centuries in which the Gospel has been held by Gentiles and given its formulation by Gentile minds using the

[25] *The Religious Pilgrimage of Israel*, 1947, pp. 255 f. The single reference to Jesus occurs in this passage.

Gentile heritage.[26] But the question with which we are now dealing, and in connection with which we cited the book by Matthews, has nothing to do with modern distortions or additions. It relates to the position of Jesus and the Apostles; it asks what the New Testament says, and what therefore the Christian student of the Old Testament may be expected to take seriously. The answer is clear, and it is emphatically stated in numerous places in the New Testament. The entire history of Israel in the pre-Christian period was under the control of the divine working which led up to and found its fulfilment in the divine work in Jesus Christ. Therefore the study of the history of Israel, and the judgment on first-century Judaism, must be undertaken in such a way that unity between the previous history, the central career of Christ, and the history of his Church is maintained.

Hence it is not possible for the convinced Christian to separate the previous history from the New Testament story, and take the former as a separate movement which finds its continuation in Judaism, while the latter is a fresh emergent which finds its continuation in the Church. The Christian Biblical scholar has no right to present the material in that way. If the previous history can properly be separated from the New Testament story, if it belongs rather to the movement which rabbinical and talmudic Judaism continues, then it is not merely the pre-Christian period which is lost from the Gospel story. It is rather the entire Gospel which is lost, for the Gospel is explicit and emphatic that its story is the continuation, the climax, and the rightful interpreting center for the previous story. If that claim is unfounded, then the Christian Gospel is quite without justification. It is an orphan in fact, and a perjurer about both its ancestry and the nature of God's working.

---

[26] The present day determination of Christians to be fair and friendly to the Jews is a splendid and thoroughly Christian thing. Through the centuries the Church has been guilty of much unkind treatment of the Jews. But neglect of essential facts is no part of friendliness.

Christian scholars who deal with the Old Testament and with the history of Israel will have to deal with the Bible as a unity. The content of the New Testament will not let them do otherwise. They will reject the New Testament position if they choose to treat the Old Testament as the rightful possession of Judaism.[27] They must interpret the Old Testament so that its relation to Christ is maintained.

IV

But how are we to explain this relation of the Old Testament to Christ? Christian scholarship at the present time is in quite a quandary on this problem. A right solution is a necessary part of the New Testament understanding of time and of the Christian attitude to Judaism.

The older method was to find everywhere in the Old Testament allegorical or at least typological references to Christ.[28] Except among quite traditionalist scholars, this method has fallen into rather general disrepute. It has been revived in a modified form by Wilhelm Vischer,[29] whose method at times seems allegorical but usually deals in typology. He declares that we find in the Old Testament the answer to the question, *What is Christ?* He then leaves it to the New Testament to tell *who* Christ is. Were he consistent in his development of this thesis —which he is not and cannot be, for the Old Testament tells a history, which Vischer takes as real history—his method would drain the Old Testament history of independent value as a constructive stage in God's redemptive program. It would also

[27] This does not deny that Judaism still retains the Old Testament. It does not question the Jew's freedom to reject Christ and use the O.T. with its talmudic rather than its N.T. interpretation. It simply states the essential Christian position that the N.T. rather than the Talmud is the true interpreting platform for the O.T.

[28] Cf. R. M. Grant, *The Bible in the Church*, 1948.

[29] *Das Christuszeugnis des Alten Testaments*, Vol. I, *Das Gesetz*, sixth ed., 1943; Vol. II, Part 1, *Die früheren Propheten*, 1942.

assume that the Old Testament was clearer about what Christ was to be than was actually the case. In fact, before the coming of Christ the Old Testament Messianic hope was not perfectly clear; of this ambiguity the New Testament itself gives evidence. The Christian can only say that Christ is attested in the Old Testament in the light of what we know him to be from the New Testament.[30] Vischer's position is therefore not satisfactory, although it is valuable as an attempt to solve a problem which too many Christian scholars simply evade.

W. J. Phythian-Adams[31] and A. G. Hebert[32] also deal with typology, but they state their method somewhat differently; they seek not only for a literal sense in Scripture but also for a spiritual sense. Both scholars, and Phythian-Adams in particular, find in the divine action in the Old Testament a fixed pattern which is repeated in the New. This method of stating the fact of fulfilment leads to or goes with a priestly conception of the Christian ministry which distorts the New Testament focus; it gives too great a place to outward form in the Old Testament, and does not do justice to the free prophetic spirit which in both Testaments is the distinctive and deepest strain.

Another solution, quite different from typology, is to trace the connection through the ascending development of ideas in

[30] The Christian, even the Christian scholar, does not come to the O.T. first and work out a complete interpretation of it before taking notice of the Gospel and the N.T. No Christian could in fact do so, nor can he find a sound theological defense for doing so. If he is a Christian, he studies as a Christian, and he will be honest and state the data of each stage of history honestly precisely because he is a Christian; he lives his whole life as a Christian. The current idea that a scholar can attain honesty and integrity only by clearing his mind of all Christian convictions is an astounding slander. If the Gospel is true, the true interpretation of the relevant documents can be given only in the light of the Gospel. Applied to the O.T., this means that only in the light of the Gospel as clearly stated in the N.T. can the O.T. be placed in its true setting and correctly interpreted.

[31] Cf. especially his book, *The Way of At-One-Ment*, 1944.

[32] Cf. *The Throne of David*, 1941; *The Authority of the Old Testament*, 1947.

Israel to Christ; this point of view has become particularly well known through its popularization in the writings of Harry Emerson Fosdick.[33] Such an approach, which contains an element of truth, does not do justice to the essential claim of both Old and New Testaments that what is basically involved is not merely revealed ideas but chiefly the action of God.

Hence other scholars emphasize that it is a record of the redemptive working of God that the entire story of the Bible forms a unity.[34] Christ then comes as the crown and climax of the Old Testament story, and the Old Testament interpreter completes his task only by showing, or clearly opening the way for the New Testament scholar to show, how this takes place. This position accepts the repeated assertion of the New Testament.

However, we still have not included the entire New Testament claim. The more the Church grew in its grasp of the greatness of what God had done in Christ, and the more Christians thought about the greatness of the work and character of Christ himself, so much the more did they see in him the eternal Son of God, in whose continuous working could be found the unifying explanation of all God's working and purpose. The clear assertion of Christ's pre-existence thus opened the way to establish his direct and continuous relation to earlier times.

Indeed, the general statement of this pre-existence or eternity of the Son is explicitly made in Col. 1.13 ff., Heb. 1, and John 1.1-18. It is undoubtedly in mind in 1 Cor. 8.6, in Phil. 2.5-11, in the Alpha and Omega description of Christ in the Book of Revelation (22.13, cf. 2.8), and in other New Testament passages. This Christological affirmation may be and has been dis-

[33] *A Guide to Understanding the Bible: The Development of Ideas Within the Old and New Testaments*, 1938.

[34] In addition to Cullmann, *op. cit.*, attention should be paid to E. Stauffer, *Die Theologie des Neuen Testaments*, 1941, which presents the N.T. message in chronological sequence, beginning with the Creation and following through to the eschatological completion of God's purpose. Cf. also S. de Dietrich, *Le dessein de Dieu*, 1945.

counted as a later addition to a much simpler preceding idea of the role of Jesus. Concerning this viewpoint two things should be said. In the first place, the Christological view which we have illustrated from New Testament writings is not a late development. It is present in Paul, who apparently held it from his conversion in the early or middle thirties.[35] It is present also in several other writers. Hence it was early and widely accepted in the Apostolic Church, and this makes it impossible to hold that the Synoptic Gospels were ignorant of or hostile to so generally accepted a position. In its essentials that position was surprisingly early. Secondly, insofar as later stages of New Testament formulation show development in the presentation of the essential view, it is relevant to note that whoever takes history as the means of divine revelation will not require the instantaneous explication of the full import of a decisive event. Just as the disciples needed several years to become clear concerning the universal reference of their faith,[36] so they required time in which to reach the full statement of Christ's eternal Sonship which satisfied them. But the acceptance of the fact and their formulation of the essential affirmation of pre-existence was early.

What might appear the logical conclusion of this formulation, however, was never worked out in the New Testament. The logical conclusion, we might be tempted to think, would have been the final declaration that the Son was as active and central

---

[35] His first extant statement of the view, in 1 Cor. 8.6, comes from the middle fifties. It is stated in a matter-of-fact way, as a conviction of long standing. O. Cullmann includes it as one of *The Earliest Christian Confessions* (Eng. tr., 1949), and hence not merely a private view of Paul; indeed, the tone of the passage is that of a statement which the writer would not expect any Christian to challenge. If Paul had not held this view from the time of his conversion, he had held it for some time, and he knew that other Christians held it. There is no hint that it was an innovation or that the other Apostles opposed him on this point.

[36] Acts 10.1-11,18 is more revealing in this matter than is Acts 15. Peter was slow to see the universal reach of the Gospel, but he came to see it, as both Acts and Gal. 2.1-10 testify.

in previous centuries as Christian faith and thought knew him
to be in the time following his earthly career. But the Church
never stated its faith in this way. The reason is not hard to
find. While Christians moved to the assertion that the Son or
Logos was God's agent in creation and in the divine action of
pre-Christian times, and while on occasion Paul could speak
fancifully of Christ as following the Israelites in the wilderness
in the form of a rock which gave water to drink (1 Cor. 10.4),
yet the new inbreaking of God into history in Jesus, and the
new situation which God's action in Jesus Christ created, were
so clear and central to Christians that they never sought to make
the pre-Christian centuries the scene of the presence and activity
of the Son in the same sense and to the same degree that they
found was the case 'in the days of his flesh' and thereafter.
They could not exclude him from those earlier times; they
rather insisted that he was related to and active in those periods;
but they regarded those earlier forms of his working as limited
and preparatory, and lacking in the depth of meaning for faith
and salvation which his earthly career and risen Lordship
possessed.

For Christian faith the great assertion was that 'in the fullness of time' God sent forth his Son to do a unique work (Gal.
4.4). The Son had been involved in the previous working of
God, but this was not the center of Christian interest or accent;
the main use of such truth was to show that what God had done
previously for man's good and salvation prepared for and
pointed to the central working in Jesus Christ. For now, in a
specific historical figure, God had done the unique thing, the
decisive thing, the adequately redemptive thing. Nothing was
permitted to cloud the centrality and significance of that historical career out of which flow the later stages of God's working. Here is a striking testimony to the New Testament sense
of advancing history as well as to its Christocentric outlook.

In the discussion of the relation of Christ to the Old Testament and Israel, we have insisted that the New Testament

regards this relation as essential. The vital link is in one divine action running through the one history which connected Israel with Jesus and the Church. The Christian Church is on the New Testament view the true heir to the heritage and Scripture of Israel. The long-range continuity has a deep root in the continuing working of the eternal Son throughout the entire providential and redemptive working of God, but the New Testament restricts the attention given to the pre-Christian era of the Son's working and lays great stress upon the historical career of Jesus and its decisive and continuing effects.

Thus, although the problems involved in interpreting the Old Testament in relation to Christ are not yet fully solved, the advance of recent study is not negligible. For one thing, the problem has been seen and faced. It is clear that Christian scholarship cannot deal with the Old Testament as an isolated book. Again, the scholars who are at work on this problem accept the critical method of study; there is no hope of advance on any other basis. Moreover, they take seriously the Canon. Much recent scholarship has not taken any clear position on this issue.[37] Furthermore, these scholars rightly believe that there is a sweep and scope in God's action during the Biblical period which the eye of faith and the cooperating mind can discern; they thus can recognize the limitation of outlook and understanding in an individual leader or author, while they hold to a wider context in which we now may see the significance and forward-looking penetration of that individual's utterances. The result is that while they see the newness and decisiveness of what only happened in 'the fullness of time' (Gal. 4.4), they can see a broad principle of promise and realization working itself out in Biblical history. They take seriously the prominent Biblical assertion that God has a purpose, that he works out that purpose in stages, that he leads men to look forward to his

[37] M. Burrows' valuable *Outline of Biblical Theology*, 1946, p. 20, accepts the Protestant canon only as approximately satisfactory in its limits.

decisive work, and that the decisive working has been and is being achieved in the work of Jesus Christ. Thus they have a deep sense of the unity of Scripture. The history of the two Testaments forms one history, and the Old Testament never finds its true and full interpretation until it is related to Christ as its goal and interpreting center.

This means that Apostolic Christianity had an unavoidable conflict with first-century Jewish leaders who rejected the claim of Christ, and the Church today has essentially the same conflict with modern Judaism, because the Christian scholar must say that in the divine intention the pilgrimage of Israel, the outlook of the Old Testament, was not to rabbinical Judaism but rather and rightly to Christ.

v

If it thus becomes clear from the New Testament that all time down to the earthly ministry of Christ is bound together by the fact of Christ, it is even clearer that all subsequent time is likewise bound to him and affected by his work and his Lordship. When Jesus is taken only as a teacher and example, he recedes ever further into the past. But when he is recognized as the risen, exalted Lord, and so as the continuing contemporary of the Church, the situation is different. Every generation is directly related to Christ, but on the basis of his first-century redemptive action.

Sometimes this relation is spoken of as the working of the risen, living Christ (Matt. 28.20; John 14.18; Acts 18.10; Rom. 8.10; Gal. 2.20). At other times he works through the Spirit. While this latter idea is not always expressed, it occurs so often that we cannot assume it to have been absent from the Church at any time.[38] The risen Christ rules as Lord through the Spirit whom he gives to his people.

[38] Chapter Three will deal in greater detail with the Holy Spirit and the Church.

In the period of the Church there is a curious tension.[39] The life of the believer does indeed have a constant tie with the contemporary Lord and Head of the Church, but it has a time framework in two other quite notable respects. Faith has a constant backward look. It has its basis and justification in God's central and decisive act in Jesus of Nazareth—his life, ministry, death, and resurrection. But the believer's life faces not so much backward as forward. With the risen Lord the believer faces forward and moves forward to the full realization of God's purpose at the end of the age.

There are those who diminish the tension between these two foci of faith's vision by minimizing the future consummation. They say that in Christ the End has come; this, stated without qualification, implies that in Christ's earthly career God finished his work. E. C. Rust, in *The Christian Understanding of History*,[40] makes this assertion, largely in dependence on C. H. Dodd and Dodd's view of realized eschatology. Then Rust has no logical place for the future eschatological drama. But he made the dilemma; the New Testament did not. He overstated the significance of the earthly career of Christ by saying that in Jesus' earthly work the end had come; then he had no clear place for the obvious forward looking and eager outlook of the Apostolic Church.

Other scholars do the opposite; they hold that the Apostles expected everything from the future.[41] The career of Christ

---

[39] See O. Cullmann, *Christ and Time*, pp. 144 ff.

[40] Published in 1947; see p. 67. On Dodd's view, see note 18. Rust rightly sees the decisive effect of the first-century work of Christ; cf. Matt. 12.28; Rom. 10.4. But he needs to distinguish more clearly between the decisive action which begins the new age and the full establishment of that new order; cf. 1 Cor. 15.23-28. He does this later in the book, but here, under the influence of a concept of eternity as a state above and independent of time, he blurs the picture by introducing a conception of the end which he implies on p. 68 has no temporal reference. To me this weakens an otherwise valuable book.

[41] M. Werner, in *Die Entstehung des Christlichen Dogmas*, 1941, underestimates the N.T. conviction that in what Christ has done the

was but a promise; apocalyptic fulfilment will bring everything, and do so soon. Here again the scholar creates his dilemma. For the New Testament finds something so decisive in the work of God in Christ that the believer must always look back to that epochal act with gratitude and increasing understanding (Gal. 1.4), even while he knows that 'he who began a good work in you will bring it to completion at the day of Jesus Christ' (Phil. 1.6 RSV).

The tension remains. The New Testament lives with it. Oscar Cullmann has grasped this and set it forth with vigor in *Christ and Time*. The time of the Church is the time in which God has begun his decisive redemption but has not yet fully completed it. This time must move forward under the Lordship of Christ until the day when Christ completes his work. For 'he must reign until he hath put all his enemies under his feet' (1 Cor. 15.25). He will defeat every hostile force and give over to God a fully established Kingdom (1 Cor. 15.28). Christ's present working gives real meaning to the present period of time, just as the preparatory working which led up to his earthly career gave actuality to time. And the perfect order of which the New Testament speaks, the perfect order which according to the New Testament has been prepared for God's people, is that which is to *follow* the present provisional reign of Christ. The New Testament never floats off into the stratosphere of timelessness to seek there a perfect bliss. Its thought, even when it speaks of the perfect order, is in terms of time. That time will be one in which 'the ages of the ages'[42] will follow in steady unending sequence. The God of that perfect order is he who is known only through his

decisive action has occurred. All hope for the future rests upon this decisive inauguration of a new and climactic stage of God's working. This puts the real basis of the Christian faith in the past work of Christ and then in the present Lordship of Christ.

[42] This expression occurs in eight N.T. books. The similar phrase 'into the age,' or 'into the ages,' with plain reference to a future period or periods, we find used in thirteen books.

progressive working in time, and for whom time therefore is real.

Thus even eschatology is expressed in terms of time. This is true first of all in the sense that eschatology begins with the earthly career of Christ.[43] The time of the Church is eschatological time insofar as the final redemptive working of God is definitely under way. Christ has redeemed us out of the present evil age; so Paul can say (Gal. 1.4), although he in company with the other New Testament writers knows that there is full redemption yet to come (2 Cor. 5.2; 2 Pet. 3.13)[44] and that therefore the present time is a time of tension. But the atmosphere of eschatology has come upon the Church; the theme of fulfilment is strong.

Yet expectancy and the attitude of waiting is equally present. While the decisive action has occurred, and the final outcome is therefore certain (Rom. 8.32), the full realization of what has been decided is yet to come. It is future. It is to come in a time sense. The perfect order is an order which will be set up in time and endure thereafter.

The Gospel of John comes nearest to dropping this expectation, but it does not really do so. With all of its strong understanding of the greatness of present Christian privilege, it still speaks of the resurrection at the last day (5.28,29, 6.39,40,44,54, 12.48) and of the final state (14.3). A number of scholars have tried to allegorize these time references,[45] but this does violence to the true meaning. Nor is it possible to excise them as later additions;[46] such an attempt only calls attention to the fact that

[43] Only for this reason can it be said that the Kingdom has in one sense come (Matt. 12.28; Col. 1.13), or that Christ is even now Lord (Acts 2.36; Phil. 2.9-11), or that Christ has brought the reign of the Law to an end for believers (Rom. 10.4), or that the old sacrificial system has been superseded (Heb. 7-10).

[44] Although 2 Pet. was the last N.T. book to be written, it did not lose this sense of a redemption to be completed in time (3.10,13).

[45] Cf. B. W. Robinson, *The Gospel of John*, 1925, pp. 198 f.

[46] R. Bultmann argues for such excision in *Das Evangelium des Johannes*, 1941.

they are present in the Gospel to resist a timeless interpretation of eternal life.[47]

VI

The New Testament is thus a time-charged book. Because the decisive redemption is effected by God in a series of specific events which find their center in Jesus Christ, time is real and the sequence of such events is essential to the Gospel.

It does not view history as a series of cycles, as did classical Greek and much Hellenistic thought, which saw no meaning or goal in time, looked to no decisive event or historical series of events for redemption, and hence could use the cycle image as appropriate.[48] It does not regard life as an annual cycle, as did the nature cults and their maturer form in many mystery cults. It does not hold, as those of mystical bent, including perhaps many mystery initiates, were inclined to do, that the

---

[47] There is thus much greater agreement between the Synoptic and Johannine outlook than is often recognized. When the Kingdom is interpreted as entirely future and eternal life as a conception without eschatological reference, the difference is radical. But when the Kingdom is seen as beginning with the work of Jesus Christ, and eternal life as including a reference to future blessing, a large and indeed basic agreement appears. T. W. Manson, in *The Teaching of Jesus*, 1931, Chap. 7, presents effectively the evidence that already in the teaching of Jesus the present reality of God's reign is set forth, in a way which allows full place for the eschatological picture in Chap. 8: 'The Final Consummation.' This is the common N.T. picture. God has acted decisively in Jesus Christ, but what he then began will find completion only in the future.

[48] On the prevalence of the theory of cycles among both Greeks and Romans see J. B. Bury, *The Idea of Progress*, 1921, pp. 10-13; he states that they regarded time as the 'enemy of humanity' and that the theory of world-cycles was practically the 'orthodox theory of cosmic time.' See also Niebuhr, *op. cit.*, pp. 38 f.; A. J. Toynbee, *A Study of History*, 1947, pp. 251 f. The Gnostic movement disliked the Hebraic and N.T. conception of history, and preferred the Greek concentration upon ideas to the Biblical emphasis upon the particularity of historical events. Essentially, the Bible rejected the Greek view in its Gnostic adaptation.

state of perfection is a timeless calm obtained by escaping the process of history and time; it conceives it rather as a goal and blessing to which all believers move under Christ the Lord and in keeping with the sovereign and gracious purpose of the God who is known precisely through his work in the sequence of historical events.

Just as this Christ-centered, time-charged view of life and redemption, for all its deep unity with the Old Testament, is not in its center and organizing principle a mere borrowing from Judaism, but a challenge whose acceptance would have involved the end of Judaism as it then was, even so it is no derivative from the Hellenistic mind and life. It is an original message derived from the career of Christ, in whose unique action faith sees the decisive and interpreting center of the historical working of God the Judge and Redeemer of men.

CHAPTER THREE

'LED BY THE SPIRIT'

I<small>N</small> thinking about 'The God and Father of our Lord Jesus Christ,' we found that the theology of the New Testament grows out of the career, the work, and the significance of Jesus Christ, who as the risen Lord of the Church gives the clue to the purpose and character of God. In thinking about 'The Fullness of Time,' we found that all of history is seen by the New Testament in the light of that career of Christ, so that he is the focus of one unified divine working which gives meaning to the history of man upon this earth.

With respect to both of these points the New Testament naturally owes much in form and expression to the Jewish background and in a lesser degree to the Hellenistic environment, but the controlling faith, the dominating thinking, is not a dependent, derived, and secondary thing, but rather a fresh creative emergent in the spiritual life of mankind. It is, in the New Testament point of view, the result of the initiating and gracious work of the holy and powerful God, working through Christ to meet the needs of men in a unique and effective manner.

I

In this third and last of our discussions, we are to think about Christian worship and daily life. When we do so, we are not moving away from the Christ-centered position which, as we have seen, characterizes the New Testament. Once we have recognized that in the New Testament Jesus Christ is the risen Lord, we are ready to recognize that the life of his people will stand constantly under his Lordship. This is true of the entire Christian life. We do not find life split into one area, of worship, where Christ is honored, and another area in which man is more independent. If we are to present the New Testament position, we can make no essential distinction between worship and daily life; the relation of the disciples to Christ covers all of life at all times. The entire life is under the Lordship of Christ and so is at his service (Luke 6.46; Rom. 12.1 f.; 1 Cor. 6.19 f.).

Yet the New Testament says with equal emphasis that the life of the disciples is led and empowered by the Holy Spirit. The gift of the Holy Spirit to believers is mentioned in anticipation in all four Gospels (e.g., Matt. 3.11; Mark 1.8; Luke 3.16; John 15.26); the realization of that expectation is reported in both John and Acts (John 20.22; Acts 2.4). The fact that the Christian life is guided and blessed by the Holy Spirit is attested in almost all of the remaining books of the New Testament (e.g., 2 Cor. 1.22, 3.3). The fact of the Spirit's presence and aid is so frequently noted in the New Testament that it obviously is a common point in the experience and teaching of the Apostolic Church. We have no evidence of a section of the Church which did not know the gift of the Spirit. There are variations in the way the Spirit is received, as in Samaria and Caesarea (Acts 8.14-17, 10.44-48), and we find a puzzling preparatory form of faith which requires further instruction, as at Ephesus (Acts 19.1-7),[1] but we learn of no branch of the Church where the gift of the Spirit had not been received. Moreover, just as in the case of the relation to the risen Christ, the relation to the Holy Spirit included all of life. The Spirit was active in worship

[1] These twelve men at Ephesus are called 'disciples' who had 'believed,' but they evidently had not been baptized 'into the name of the Lord Jesus,' for Paul proceeds to do that. They had been baptized 'into John's baptism,' and since Apollos upon arrival at Ephesus knew 'only the baptism of John,' so that Priscilla and Aquila 'expounded unto him the way of God more accurately' (18.25 f.), they most likely were converted by Apollos. The situation was unique. See K. Lake and H. J. Cadbury, *The Beginnings of Christianity, Part I, The Acts of the Apostles*, Vol. 4, English Translation and Commentary, 1933, *in loco*.

(Rom. 8.26 f.; 1 Cor. 12), in group relationships (Eph. 2.18-22), and in personal endeavour (Acts 4.8; Rom. 8.14).[2]

What then is the relation between the risen Christ, the Lord of the Church, and the Holy Spirit who is given to the Church? The comprehensive relation of both Christ and the Spirit to all phases of life indicates that the relation between the two was close indeed. This fact receives emphasis when we note that there are passages where it is difficult to distinguish the two. For example, in Romans 8.9-11, the divine Spirit is successively called 'the Spirit,' 'the Spirit of God,' 'the Spirit of Christ,' 'Christ,' and 'the Spirit of him that raised up Jesus from the dead.' Similarly, in 2 Cor. 3.17, we read that 'the Lord is the Spirit: and where the Spirit of the Lord is, there is liberty.'

Yet the two are not identified. Some scholars have insisted that in the passages just cited there is such identification,[3] but this is an unreasonable assertion, for in those very letters there are other passages where the Spirit and Christ are treated as separate in some way (Rom. 15.18 f.; 2 Cor. 3.3, 13.14). The two are closely linked without being identified.

What prevents Paul and others from making the identification? It is not hard to answer. The memory of the historical career of Jesus Christ is too vivid and too influential to permit the fusing of the living Christ with the Holy Spirit in Christian thought and worship. He who ministered, died, and rose, continues to live, and his continuing life is so tied to his earthly career that he cannot be taken as identical with the Holy Spirit.[4]

[2] The N.T. does not say that the Holy Spirit guides isolated individuals. The specific persons and special ministries prompted and supported by the Spirit are to be understood as working within the fellowship of the Church. The distinction between group direction and individual guidance is likely to be misleading.

[3] E.g., J. Knox, *Christ the Lord*, 1941, p. 66. See E. Andrews, *The Meaning of Christ for Paul*, 1949, pp. 147 ff., for an answer to Knox.

[4] It seems quite improbable that Paul thought of Christ as a 'fluctuating power' or a 'penetrating divine fluid.' This assertion of J. Weiss, *The History of Primitive Christianity*, Eng. Tr., 1937, Vol. II, p. 484, ascribes to Paul too impersonal a conception of Christ.

Moreover, the influence of the historical career is so strong that it not only prevents the Christian view from absorbing the living Christ into the Spirit, but actually determines the work of the Spirit, whose role is to continue and broaden the work of the earthly Christ. It is always taken for granted in the New Testament that the work of the Holy Spirit will be consistent with and will constitute an extension of the work of Jesus (1 Cor. 12.3).

This becomes explicit in the dramatic method of the Fourth Gospel. The Paraclete or Counselor, it is said, will bring to remembrance all that Jesus has spoken (14.26); he will bear witness to Jesus (15.26); he will take the things of Christ and declare them unto the disciples (16.14); and he will convict the world of its sin in not believing in Jesus (16.8 f.). What the Fourth Gospel thus dramatically indicates, however, is the general position of the New Testament; the Spirit's work is consistent with and a continuation of the work of Jesus.

But this is not all. The living Christ sends the Spirit. This too is so frequently found a statement that it must represent the view of the Apostolic Church generally. All four of the Gospels say that Jesus will send the Holy Spirit (John 15.26, 16.7, cf. 14.16,26) or will baptize his followers with the Spirit (Matt. 3.11; Mark 1.8; Luke 3.16; cf. Acts 1.5). In thus speaking, the Synoptic Gospels indirectly indicate that they know the Pentecost story in some form. The evangelists, when they included the confident promise, knew that it had been fulfilled after the Ressurection.[5] The Fourth Gospel explicitly narrates the gift

[5] Luke showed genuine theological insight, and not merely literary skill, when he combined in the one writing Luke-Acts the story about Jesus and the work of the Spirit in the Church. The risen Christ carries forward (Acts 2.33) what he had begun. It is really one story. I have heard it suggested that the lost ending of Mark (the view of R. H. Lightfoot, *Locality and Doctrine in the Gospels*, n.d., pp. 1-48, that Mark ended at 16.8, seems plausible only because when we read 16.1-8 we read into it a further content known to us from the other Gospels)

of the Spirit by the living Christ and says that the event occurred on the evening of the resurrection day (20.19,22); it thus portrays in dramatic form what the rest of the New Testament agrees or implies was true.   Acts dates the actual gift of the Spirit a few weeks later (2.1), and this is no doubt the literal fact; but Peter in the Pentecost sermon states explicitly that the risen, exalted Christ sent the Spirit (2.33).   Paul does not clearly say this, but speaks of the Spirit as the Spirit of Christ (Rom. 8.9), as does 1 Peter (1.11).   In the Book of Revelation the Lamb's seven eyes are the seven Spirits of God (5.6);[6] this indicates that he sends forth the Spirits 'into all the earth.'   Moreover, the risen Christ speaks in the letters to the seven churches in this book, and the reader is urged to hear what the Spirit is saying to the churches in these letters (e.g., 2.1,7).   The Book therefore implies that Christ speaks and acts through the Spirit.

It is important to note that the gift of the Spirit is regarded in the New Testament as an eschatological gift.   This viewpoint is so different from the prevailing thought of the modern Christian Church that it should be emphasized.

The promise in the Synoptic Gospels that Christ will give the Spirit must be read in the light of the preaching of the Baptist and of Jesus[7] that the Kingdom is at the threshold (Matt. 3.2, 4.17; Mark 1.15).   The new order is at hand, and the reference is not merely to a new civilization or a new period of the same sort of world history, but to God's new order, estab-

contained an account of the gift of the Spirit promised in 1.8.   This is not impossible, but remains conjecture, and obscures the originality of Luke's total outline.

[6] The Book of Revelation speaks of the seven Spirits (1.4; 3.1; 4.5; 5.6) and also of 'the Spirit' (e.g., 2.7; 14.13; 22.17).   The former appears to be a symbolic reference to the fullness of the Spirit.

[7] The view of C. H. Dodd, *Parables of the Kingdom*, 1936, pp. 44 f., that Mark 1.15 means 'the Kingdom of God has come,' obscures the future note, as has been pointed out, for example, by C. T. Craig, 'Realized Eschatology,' *JBL*, Vol. 59, pp. 367 ff.

lished by divine power as the climax of God's dealings with this world.

Similarly, in Acts 2.16 the gift of the Spirit is connected with the prediction in Joel 2.28-32 that in the last days the Spirit will be given. The fact that in the Greek text of Acts usually followed the reference to 'the last days' is not found in Joel[8] shows that to the writer of Acts the phrase is no meaningless item, but is rather inserted precisely because the Apostolic Church regarded the gift of the Spirit as an eschatological event. Pentecost therefore has an eschatological quality which modern interpretation of Acts frequently fails to mention.

Another example of the same eschatologically oriented attitude is Paul's reference to the gift of the Spirit as the ' first-fruits ' (Rom. 8.23) and the ' earnest,' the first instalment of God's great climactic gifts to his people (2 Cor. 1.22, 5.5; Eph. 1.14). It is necessary to feel the eschatological atmosphere which the words ' first-fruits ' and ' earnest ' breathe in these Pauline passages; Pentecost opened the final age.

Whence came this eschatological note in the New Testament view of the Spirit? Evidently it resulted from the conviction of believers that what God had done in Christ was so decisive that the new order had been inaugurated. It had not been fully established, but those who by faith lived with Christ no longer had their life center in the old order. They already had a place in the partial and provisional stage of the final divine order. The view gives us another reflection of the common New Testament faith that the decisive event of all time was the work of Christ.

In this provisional stage we find the Church. To the believer it was beyond all question the Church of Christ. But, as Acts makes clear, it is equally the Church of the Spirit; in it the

---

[8] Joel has ' afterward,' or ' after these things ' (LXX). This refers back to the preceding paragraph, which has been speaking of future blessings which God will give, so the explicit eschatological interpretation of Acts 2.17 has some basis. Codex Vaticanus and some other textual evidence, however, agree with the LXX.

Christian is to live the life that is 'led by the Spirit' (Gal. 5.18; Rom. 8.14).

This life is no hermit existence; it is a life in the fellowship of the Church. This is clear from many points of view. First of all, New Testament thought which deals with the Kingdom of God has to do with an essentially social life. Of course the primary relationship is with God; indeed, the Greek word *basileia*, Kingdom, basically means the sovereignty and reign of God as Lord and King. But God is Father and King[9] of his people, not of isolated individuals.[10]

In the same way, the risen Lord is Lord of his people, and the thought that faith in Christ leaves fellowship in the Church optional would have been rejected by the New Testament Christians as a startling mistake. We have often taken the Pauline phrase 'in Christ' to be nothing more than an expression of individualistic mysticism. This is radically wrong; it is a view which springs from modern individualism and Greek attitudes rather than from a true understanding of the Apostle. He is clear that to be 'in Christ,' while it is a great personal experience and privilege, is a privilege which inevitably puts a man into the Church and binds him to his fellow-believers in the one 'body of Christ' (1 Cor. 12.27), of which the risen Christ is the living Head (Col. 1.18; Eph. 1.22 f.).

Similarly, the Holy Spirit is a Church-building, fellowship-building power. In Acts the Spirit comes to groups of believers, not to self-sufficient individuals.[11] The Spirit leads to united

[9] These two terms are incongruous to many moderns. But as we are reminded by the Jewish Prayer Book, which preserves much ancient usage and repeatedly contains the double address: 'Our Father, our King,' Jesus and his fellow-Jews felt no such incongruity.

[10] In two respects the phrase 'Kingdom of God' is superior to 'eternal life' as an expression of the theme of Jesus' message. It clearly states the sovereign rule of God and it also implies a life lived in relation to God's other servants. It excludes both humanism and pure individualism.

[11] Note the use of 'all,' as in 2.4, 4.31, and of the plural, as in 8.17. When an individual is in mind, as in 9.17, the gift is given within the context of the Church.

evangelistic witness and to healing, sacrificial service. The gifts of the Spirit to the Church are so varied that through his work-ing the entire Church has the ministries it needs for full fellow-ship and life (1 Cor. 12.4 ff.). The first 'fruit of the Spirit' is love (Gal. 5.22), which is unselfish fellowship in action. Paul was saying what the entire Church believed when he said that if any man does not have the Spirit of Christ, he does not belong to Christ (Rom. 8.9). We sometimes hear this verse interpreted as though by the word 'Spirit' Paul meant the inner attitude of the Christian himself, but this is wrong; the reference is rather to the Holy Spirit who links the life to Christ. Without the Spirit there is no Church and no Christian. Outside of the Spirit-built Church there is no Christian. The Church is the Church of the Spirit.

This inevitably implies what the New Testament indicates (e.g., Heb. 6.4), that the Holy Spirit is given to all believers. To be sure, it is likewise true that chosen individuals are given the Spirit for specific tasks. But this does not mean that some are left without the Spirit. Each is given the Spirit and through the Spirit some spiritual gift for the common good (1 Cor. 12.7). This again reflects the eschatological mood of the New Testa-ment. Israel had not claimed to have the universal gift of the Spirit. That was expected in the last days.[12] The Church declares that this expectation has been fulfilled. God has given his Spirit to all believers so that all are 'led by the Spirit'.

Characteristic of the New Testament gift of the Spirit is the fact that it enriches but does not replace the human experience and ability. It is particularly important to note this because so much has been made of both the speaking with tongues at Pentecost (Acts 2) and the unintelligible speech at Corinth (1 Cor. 12-14). These occurrences might suggest that all Christians who received the Spirit were deprived of

---

[12] Cf. W. Bousset, *Die Religion des Judentums im späthellenistischen Zeitalter*, third ed., edited by H. Gressmann, 1926, p. 394.

their normal faculties and dependent solely upon superhuman direction.

Highly emotional scenes there certainly were, and excesses undoubtedly occurred. But they have been over-emphasized. In the first place, the Pentecost scene appears to have been shaped in the telling, in order to bring out the point that the Gospel is for men of all countries and tongues. Even so, the real point of the story is not the emotion or the tongues, but the fact that in the presence and working of the Spirit the Church henceforth has the power and direction for its active task. In this power and impetus to active service we have the real point of the narrative. In the second place, the situation at Corinth, while confused, was not all madness. There was a minority proud of its ability to give a spectacular expression of primitive Christian joy, but there were others given to more sober and fruitful expressions of the Spirit's presence, and Paul was vigorously on the side of the latter majority group.

When we take the New Testament as a whole and listen to the writers and leaders, it is clear that the Spirit enriches but does not cancel or replace human capacities. The emotion is given a vital place, which the exaggerated intellectual emphasis of many Protestants today does not adequately value. Yet the intelligence is recognized as essential. Jesus challenges men to think and judge for themselves (cf. e.g., Luke 12.57). Paul, too, appeals to the judgment of his readers, and when he says that he would rather say five intelligible words in order to help others than speak ten thousand words in an unknown tongue (1 Cor. 14.19), he comes down solidly on the side of intelligence in the Spirit-led life.

But it is not only emotion and intelligence which are given their due. Personal responsibility, too, is enriched rather than thwarted by the work of the Spirit. It baffles many students that the good life can be called the life of the Spirit and also the responsible life of the human person. This appears to be a contradiction, and it is sometimes dismissed as sheer Calvinism.

This is a compliment to Calvinism, for the presence of both truths marks the New Testament as well.

So far as I know no human thinker has completely reconciled the sovereign working of God through his Spirit with the responsible and free working of man under God. However, unless one is to make God less than God or man less than truly human, both workings are facts, and God's working is the superior working. This is precisely what I find in the New Testament. When led by the Spirit man becomes truly free and his responsibility becomes something other than the basis on which he receives damnation for his sinful life (Gal. 5.1,13,14). Thus man's personal powers and responsibility are enriched rather than effaced in the life of the Spirit.

We have already observed that all of life is under the Spirit's guidance. We have noted that the fellowship of Christians is the inevitable result of the Spirit's working. We should likewise recognize that the worship of the believer is not the independent and purely human act which we might suppose. While the New Testament often pays no specific attention to the Spirit's prompting in worship, the fact of such divine leading finds mention in more than one way. In Acts the Spirit makes the worship really vital and effective not merely for feeling but also for life (e.g., 4.31, 9.31, 13.2). In Paul it is not only faith that is the gift of God (Eph. 2.8); the Spirit teaches us what to pray and prays in effective manner even when we cannot frame the words (Rom. 8.15,26); and whenever we get the picture of a worshipping Church, as at Corinth, the Spirit prompts the various aspects of the worship (1 Cor. 12,14). In the Fourth Gospel, as we have seen, the Spirit interprets the work of Christ and guides the thoughts and lives of the believers. Thus all of the fellowship of the Christians, and specifically their worship together, is led by the Spirit.

So also the moral obedience of the Christians is the expression of the Spirit's working. The strong protest which Jesus made when his exorcisms were charged to the working of Beelzebul[13] was due to the fact that he knew his entire ministry and life to be the result and expression of the Spirit which was in him. The sacrifices of the wealthy Christians in Acts were the result of the work of the Spirit in the Church.[14] In the letters of Paul the redeeming grace of God through Christ frees the believer not only from the guilt of sin, but also from its grip on his life, and so he can and should produce 'the fruit of the Spirit' in his life (Gal. 5.1, 13, 16, 22 f., 25). This fruit Paul describes as 'love, joy, peace, long-suffering, kindness, goodness, faithfulness, meekness, self-control' (Gal. 5.22 f.). The life led by the Spirit is a life made possible by divine grace, but it is not a lax life which trifles with the gifts of God; on the contrary, it is a life of moral obedience which the Spirit of God makes possible (Rom. 8.2-17).

II

Thus far we have attempted to describe the New Testament view of the Christian life as lived in the Church and 'led by the Spirit.' It is now our task to inquire how far this New Testament position was derived from its environment.

[13] Matt. 12.24-32; Mark 3.21-30; Luke 11.15-20. The Synoptics vary in their material and placing of it (cf. A. E. J. Rawlinson, *St. Mark*, second ed., 1927, pp. 42-45). Mark clearly indicates (3.29) that the Beelzebul charge is taken as blasphemy against the Holy Spirit in Jesus. So does Matt. in vv. 31 f., and in v. 28 he has already referred to the Spirit as operative in Jesus. This latter verse Luke parallels in 11.20, but instead of the reference to the Spirit he speaks of 'the finger of God' (cf. Ex. 8.19); moreover, the saying concerning blasphemy he has in another context (12.10). Yet in all three Gospels the vigorous reaction against the Beelzebul charge states or implies that the Spirit is working through Jesus.

[14] Acts 4.32-37 follows immediately the statement that the praying disciples were filled with the Spirit. Moreover, 5.3 implies that in handling property the believer is related to the Spirit and responsible to him for integrity of action.

F

In many respects the kinship with the Old Testament and with Judaism is apparent. Insofar as the Jewish outlook anticipated the eschatological gift of the Spirit,[15] there was a preparation for a prominent aspect of the New Testament picture. Again, the strong sense of belonging to a chosen people of God is found in the Old Testament; it marked Judaism; it leaves its deep mark on the New Testament.[16]   Furthermore, the wholesome insistence upon obedience to the will of God, an accent which we find stressed in both the law (Lev. 18.5) and the prophets (Isa. 1.16 f.; Ezek. 20.11; Amos 5.24; Micah 6.8), continues to exercise strong influence (Mark 3.35; John 7.17; Eph. 6.6; Heb. 13.21; 1 John 2.17), and no Protestant stress upon the free grace of God should be allowed to obscure the continuance of that insistence in the New Testament message. Finally, the insight that the religious relation encompasses and controls *all* of life, and not merely special times of worship or observance, is a prophetic inheritance which found one embodiment in Pharisaism and was a heritage handed on to Christianity by the Scripture and life of Israel (1 Cor. 10.31; Col. 3.17).   Thus kinship and dependence are obvious in the relation of the New Testament to the Old Testament and Judaism.

1. Nevertheless, it cannot be said that the creative center and the vital content of this Spirit-led life is derived from Judaism. In the first place, this life is of such a nature that it necessarily excludes the rule of an authoritative code of law.   While Christians sometimes understand the legal regime of Judaism in too rigid a way, it remains true that the revealed will of God, embodied in his law and in the legal framework of life, exercised a commanding control which the rule of the Spirit does

[15] See note 12.

[16] The Greek term *ho laos*, used in the LXX and N.T. of the Jews as 'the people' specially related to God, as contrasted with *ta ethnē*, 'the (remaining) nations' or Gentiles, is applied to the Christians with definite inclusion of Gentile disciples in this new people of God.   See, e.g., Acts 15.14, 18.10; Rom. 9.25 f.; Heb. 13.12; 1 Pet. 2.9; Rev. 18.4.

not permit.[17]   When Paul said that Christ is the end of the
law to everyone who believes (Rom. 10.4), some interpreters
think that he was quite arbitrarily setting a terminus to the
legal era.   But the delimiting was not arbitrary.   Paul saw that
the terminus was inherent in the decisive action of God in
Christ, and that a new order was present in the rule which
Christ the risen Lord was exercising through the Holy Spirit
which he had sent to guide and empower the life of believers
in the Church.

Thus in the New Testament the center of control is no longer
in the law.   That law was a preparation for Christ, and he
'fulfilled' it as he did the entire Scripture; it was Scripture and
set forth the will of God; but the effective life of God's people is
no longer regulated and framed by law as it had been before
Rom. 6.14).[18]   Even the eschatological expectation which
Judaism held concerning the gift of the Spirit is not adequate
to explain the rise of this Church which knew itself to be 'led
by the Spirit.'   The vital point of origin was a historical action,
the career of Jesus Christ and the gift of the Spirit, which
Judaism, in denying to it any crucial or constructive significance,
denied was of divine origin.

2. Involved in this rejection of the legal framework of life
was the rejection of the right of oral tradition to control worship and conduct.   As we noted in our first chapter, the Torah

---

[17] The Pentateuch played in Judaism a role which Christians often
underestimate. It was the Scripture *par excellence*. Around it centered
the worship and practice of Judaism. Note that Philo's commentaries
deal with the Pentateuch, and until the logic of his method is understood,
one has not understood Judaism. G. F. Moore, *Judaism*, Vol. I, p. 239,
stresses this fact, calling the other sacred books 'an authority of the
second rank.'

[18] The N.T. stress upon love as the summary (Mark 12.28-31) or the
fulfilment (Rom. 13.8-10; Gal. 5.14, cf. Jas. 2.8) of the law shifts the
center of life from conformity to inwardly motivated obedience. The
Pharisaic teaching that certain matters were left to the heart, and so not
reduced to commandments, resembles the N.T. position, but is still
subject to the legal framework of life.

to the Pharisee was not simply the written Pentateuch, but the Pentateuch plus the authoritative oral tradition. Jesus and the Pharisees had a clash over the validity of this tradition; he denied that it had the binding character which the Pharisees claimed for it (cf. Mark 7.5-9).[19] In this his disciples naturally followed him,[20] and thereby continued the position which had involved Jesus in a break with the spiritual leadership of the Pharisees in Judaism.

It must not be thought that the disciples had no place for tradition. We soon find Paul speaking of Christian traditions which must be preserved (1 Cor. 11.2; 2 Thess. 2.15; cf. Jude 3). But the reference is to traditions concerning the career and work of Christ and the meaning of that career for Christian faith, and there was no slavish adherence to the form of the tradition.[21] It was subject to the event which had happened in Christ, and the guidance of the Spirit led to both a respect for and an interpretation of that event. The Christians thus rejected the tradition which the Pharisees held as important, and their own tradition was subject to the event of Christ and the work of the Spirit. Neither in content nor in organizing principle did this position derive from Judaism.

[19] In this Marcan passage Jesus goes on to attack the Corban practice. Later rabbis likewise attacked the practice Jesus condemned; cf. the Mishnah tractate Nedarim 9.1 in H. Danby, *The Mishnah*, 1933, p. 275, and see Montefiore, *The Synoptic Gospels*, Vol. I, pp. 148-52. Did Jesus' criticism have a wholesome effect? While some Pharisees quite likely agreed with him, the passage clearly reflects a first-century practice which later rabbis disowned. In our discussion this is a minor point. The Pharisaic defense of the authority of their oral tradition is not in question in a discussion as to whether the Corban practice was included in that tradition.

[20] The Judaizers, who fought Paul but were essentially disowned by the Jerusalem leaders (Gal. 2.9; Acts 15.1-29), certainly maintained the necessity of keeping the law or at least certain test requirements in it, but it is not clear that even they asserted the binding character of the oral tradition.

[21] It was out of these traditions that the Gospels developed and the Epistles drew their basic teaching. The variations in parallel passages in the Synoptic Gospels show that there was no rigid fixity of form.

3. It is equally true that the Christian life in the Spirit broke with the priestly framework of Judaism. It is noteworthy that even in the Old Testament, where the priesthood is so honored, it is the prophetic element which controls.[22] In the work of John the Baptist and Jesus, the priestly element is again subordinated to the prophetic accent. The same attitude characterizes the apostolic writings generally.

Even in the Epistle to the Hebrews, which sounds so much like an apology for the priestly way of worship and life, the imagery of sacrifice and priesthood is used to show that the Old Testament priestly order was not really effective (10.4.), and that the ministry of Christ ends that priestly order (10.9). The sequel to the Old Testament priesthood in Hebrews is not a New Testament order of priests, ministering on behalf of Christ, but rather the ministry which Christ, the one eternal high priest, carries on in the heavenly sanctuary (7.25 f., 8.1 f., 9.11 ff.). Hebrews knows absolutely nothing of a human priesthood in the Church; it rather stands against the possibility of such an order. Hence while, as 1 Peter indicates (2.9; cf. Rev. 1.6), the work of Christ may suggest a priestly line of thought, and the N.T. makes figurative use of priestly imagery, the real unique mediation is that of Christ, and the universal priesthood of believers, which is the antithesis of a priestly hierarchy, is the corollary of this unique role of Christ.

Sacrifice too is reinterpreted, as it had already begun to be reinterpreted in Judaism, in a wider spiritual and moral sense (e.g., Rom. 12.1 f.). However, the Christian rejection of the priestly framework of Judaism is more radical than the beginnings of such rejection in Judaism, so it is not possible to explain satisfactorily this aspect of the New Testament from Jewish trends. The radical New Testament development roots in an event which had so decisive a meaning that it was soon seen to

[22] The substantial 'prophetic' content in the Pentateuch should not be overlooked. Law and prophets shared a common concern for the will of God and moral obedience by man.

have ended the role of animal sacrifices, as well as the possibility of strict priestly mediation by one man for another. When the rough hand of Rome ended the temple sacrifices in A.D. 70, Judaism survived because the synagogue provided a basis, but necessity gave them no such theological ground for discarding the temple rites as the act of God in Christ had already given the Christians. Their life led by the Spirit could not be fitted into the priestly framework of Judaism.

4. The fact that the Spirit was given to Gentiles as well as Jews, for example in the Cornelius household (Acts 10.44) and in the churches of Galatia (Gal. 3.2), was not beyond the outlook of Jewish eschatological expectation, but the giving of the Spirit without regard to keeping of the law, and the insistence that the Spirit had already been given in a first stage of eschatological drama, constituted features of the Christian outlook and life which were unacceptable to the Judaism of the day. The impulse to such a type of life is not traceable to traditional Jewish sources, but is connected with a series of events which center in Jesus.

Indeed, the entire eschatological hope, as we have noted, is tied to a historical figure and event in which contemporary Judaism saw imposture rather than fulfilment. Insofar as Judaism lived in hope, that hope was based on past events and promises other than the central event in Christ.[23] Moreover, the Jewish hope still awaited fulfilment. The last days had not come, nor begun to come.[24] The inevitable conclusion from all of these comparisons is that the Christian experience and doctrine of the Holy Spirit, and of the life in which the believer is 'led by the Spirit,' is not at heart a borrowing from Jewish sources. The extensive indebtedness to the Old Testament and to Judaism was utilized in the service of a faith rooted in

---

[23] In Jewish thought the Exodus was the great redemption and pre-figured the decisive final redemptive act of God.

[24] Cf. Cullmann, *Christ and Time,* in which this vital difference is stressed.

the specific history of Christ, and this event and its Christian interpretation controlled the inherited material.

III

We turn to the question whether Gentile influences exercised any decisive influence on the conception of the Spirit and the Spirit-led life. The comparison here is naturally more difficult to sum up in a brief compass, since the Gentile environment extended so far and had so varied a form.

1. One large area of Gentile life, to which we pointed in the first chapter, may be summed up in the word polytheism.[25] In contrast with such polytheistic religion, Christian faith and life possessed a vital unity under the one God who acted in Christ and sends his Spirit.

The worship of many gods was distracting by reason of the very number of deities whom the worshipper had to attempt to please. The situation must often have involved the polytheist in what labor unions call 'jurisdictional disputes,' for more than one god might claim attention at a given time. If it is impossible to serve two masters (Matt. 6.24), how could the polytheist find inner peace or consistency of life? It was not merely a matter of meeting the claims, perhaps conflicting, of known deities. One might offend an unknown God (cf. Acts 17.23)[26] or fail to find help because of ignorance of the one deity who could give the needed boon.

[25] I come back to polytheism because although it was the prevailing situation in the Gentile world and even received outward conformity from many advanced thinkers of the first century, we find little attention paid to the theology and ethic of the polytheist. How did his polytheism shape his worship and life? What is said above gives only a glance at the complex situation, which needs more attention.

[26] For a discussion of literary references and a possible inscription dealing with unknown gods, see F. J. Foakes Jackson and K. Lake, *The Beginnings of Christianity, Part I, The Acts of the Apostles*, Vol. V, 1933, note 19, 'The Unknown God,' pp. 240-46.

Moreover, who was to say which god's claim had precedence at a given time? Perhaps custom, perhaps the worshipper himself must decide. In other words, the polytheist or his group tended to become the arbiter of the competing claims of many gods. This was bound to yield an inadequate and unworthy religious life.

From such distraction, conflict, fear, and human self-assertion the faith in the Christian God delivered believers. Life received unity and all life was taken into the Spirit's control. The religious life led by the Spirit has a depth and richness which are utterly different from the distraction or the crafty calculation of polytheism.

2. A special form of polytheism was the emperor worship whose beginnings date earlier than the Apostolic Age, but whose radical challenge to the new faith became clear only at the end of the New Testament period. The Book of Revelation shows the clash at its clearest, but the Fourth Gospel may reflect it in its climax, when Thomas says to Jesus, ' My Lord and my God ' (John 20.28). Since Domitian liked to be called ' Lord and God,' *Dominus et Deus*,[27] this Gospel may be saying, It is not Domitian but Jesus Christ who is our Lord and God; he is the true Lord and God.

It is obvious that Christianity owed nothing essential to such emperor worship. Nor was it indebted in the least to that practical atheism such as the Epicureans professed, in which the gods are remote, unconcerned, and practically irrelevant. The teaching that the Spirit guides every aspect of the life of both

[27] According to Suetonius' life of Domitian, Section 13, in *Lives of the Caesars*, Book 8. The above suggestion is most probable if the Gospel is dated around A.D. 95. Recent papyrus discoveries indicate that it cannot be dated much later; cf. C. H. Roberts, *An Unpublished Fragment of the Fourth Gospel in the John Rylands Library*, 1935; H. I. Bell and T. C. Skeat, *Fragments of an Unknown Gospel and Other Early Christian Papyri*, 1935; G. Mayeda, *Das Leben-Jesu-Fragment Papyrus Egerton 2 und seine Stellung in der urchristlichen Literaturgeschichte*, 1946.

the Church and the individual Christian is the very reverse of such a view.

3. Since Christ is Lord, the Gentile cults of 'gods many and lords many' (1 Cor. 8.6) has seemed to some scholars to be not only a parallel but even a source of the religious worship found in the New Testament. We saw in the first of these three chapters how little basis there is for deriving from the pagan cults the Christian faith in Jesus Christ as the risen Lord. Just now our point is somewhat different. When such pagan lords were the objects of worship and entreaty, they were rarely deities who governed the daily life of the adherent in every aspect.[28] There occurs in them little real parallel to the Christian experience of the Spirit as the ever-present guide and power of life. This fact shows that the Christian worship and ethic is quite different from most pagan worship of lords, and it confirms the earlier conclusion that when the Lord Christ is compared with the pagan lords, the differences are deep and decisive.

4. In one significant area of Gentile life there was a teaching of the indwelling divine nature which appears to parallel the Christian doctrine of the Spirit and the Spirit-led life. This, of course, is the Logos teaching, and the Stoic development of it in particular.[29] Up to a point the parallel holds good, and the fact that Philo made so much use of the Logos concept in his Biblical interpretation suggests that we have here one of the closest parallels to Christian teaching which the pagan world

[28] The pagan cults were not exclusive and intolerant of competitors, as were Judaism and Christianity. They were open to polytheistic practice, except insofar as the view gained ground that all religions worship the same one God. This view discredits all existing religions, or at least all but one, as unworthy and misleading, and it tends too persistently to justify polytheism or gloss over its weaknesses. It lacks a strong word of judgment on man's perversions of God's revelation. See S. Angus, *The Mystery Religions and Christianity*, pp. 244 ff., 277 ff.

[29] On the Logos in Greek, O.T., and Jewish thought, as well as in the N.T., see G. Kittel, *Theologisches Woerterbuch zum N.T.*, Vol. 4, pp. 69 ff. On Philo see also Wolfson, *Philo*, Vol. I, Chaps. 4 and 6.

can supply. When one reads Col. 1.13-23 and Heb. 1.1-4, as well as the less developed passage 1 Cor. 8.6, the parallel comes to mind, and when the Prologue of the Fourth Gospel makes it explicit, the result is impressive.

But it is not a full parallel. In the Christian presentation, the Christian teaching does not confuse the divine spark with the human soul, as Stoic thought tended to do. In the second place, the Son or Logos is more personal than in the Stoic or even the Philonic version. Moreover, to the Christian the Son or Logos is uniquely connected with a single human life (John 1.14) in a way which is unknown to the Stoics and is not really paralleled by Philo's tendency to think of the Logos as specially present in Moses. Furthermore, the Cross, the redemptive work of the Son or Logos, is central in the Christian view, and this is not paralleled in the Stoic or Philonic view. Finally, in the Christian account the Son or Logos is linked with the historical Christ and not, as logic would lead us to expect, with the Spirit. This most notable difference is striking, but it is often overlooked. The fact shows that the Christian doctrine of the Spirit is not a borrowing from Stoic sources, either directly or indirectly. It derives from a historical career and its sequel, rather than from a Greek philosophy.

5. A feature of much Gentile religious life and thinking which the Christian Gospel contradicts is the dualism between matter and spirit. Where this dualism is taken seriously, the physical life is a handicap and has no positive place in the spiritual life. Some self-indulgent persons took courage from such dualism to live sensual lives; since the body had no place in the spiritual life, what one did with it made no difference; one could be spiritually pure and good regardless of physical indulgence or excess. Others, of more serious mind, felt obligated to crush the physical impulses as far as possible. The logic of their position would have been suicide, but they inconsistently clung to physical existence and sought to keep it under control by ascetic practices.

The Christian was saved from such sensuality or asceticism by his inherited understanding that the God of grace was also the Creator, who had made the world, and saw that it was 'very good' (Gen. 1.31). The body was his creation even as was the soul. The body was to be controlled but it was not to be despised. Hence Christ can come in the flesh (John 1.14; Heb. 5.7) without sin. Hence his followers are to be pure in physical life. Their bodies can be temples of the Holy Spirit (1 Cor. 6.19), a view utterly excluded for the large areas of Greek thought which operated under the influence of such dualism. The body and the whole man can be presented as a living sacrifice (Rom. 12.1 f.), and the fruit of the Spirit can be self-control (Gal. 5.23). There is here a unity of life, a physical and psychological soundness and a spiritual wholesomeness, which puts to shame all dualism between matter and spirit.

6. The life of the believer who is 'led by the Spirit' differs also from that of the Gnostic[30] who prides himself on his aristocracy of knowledge. To be sure, the developed Gnosticism which threatened the second-century Church must not be dated back into the New Testament period. But the tendencies were already present. The idea began to appear that a revealed 'knowledge' could save, and that such knowledge was available to those who were 'spiritual.' The common herd were beyond the pale; salvation was not for them.

This tendency contradicts the Christian accent, which sees man's basic problem not in ignorance but in sin and in the resulting need of a power capable of transforming the perverted nature of man. Sinful man does not need merely to know the right answers and techniques; he needs a radical change of his nature and attitudes, so that he is free from the grip of evil and is willingly led by the Spirit of God, whose power and guidance will keep him safe.

This Gnostic tendency also contradicts Christian universal-

[30] See S. Angus, *Religious Quests of the Graeco-Roman World*, Chap. 20.

ism, by which I mean the inclusiveness which offers the Gospel to all men of all classes and does not count any man to be outside the pale. The Gnostic aristocracy of special knowledge has neither the concern for 'publicans and sinners' (Luke 15.1) nor the 'whosoever' note (Rom. 10.13) which marks the Christian Gospel. As a result, it cannot parallel the Christian experience that the leading of the Spirit results in new life, willing obedience and broadly inclusive fellowship.

7. Characteristic of certain pagan cults was frenzy and extreme emotionalism. Symptoms of over-emphasis on emotional aspects of spiritual worship appear occasionally in Christianity, as in the speaking with tongues at Corinth, but such tendencies were generally brought under control of the common faith, and responsible leaders met excess with condemnation. By and large, the impression which the New Testament leaves is that the worship and life of the Apostolic Church displayed more emotion than the average liberal Protestant Church of to-day. In view of the widely admitted weakness of present-day Protestantism, the difference is not automatic proof of the inferiority of the New Testament. In any case, we have seen that the control of emotionalism by intelligence and moral responsibility is present in the New Testament. Certainly the experience of the Spirit and the joy at the Spirit's presence and guidance cannot be derived from the pagan cults in which frenzy and at times immorality played so large a part. Such Christian expressions of the Spirit-lifted life appear early, among Jews as well as Gentiles, and in reaction to the Primitive Christian message.

8. Somewhat related to the experience of frenzy, but not identical with it, is the mystical absorption which some religious Gentiles sought.[31] This was undoubtedly a minor tendency in the total scene of pagan life, but it was the goal of some of

---

[31] *Ibid.*, pp. 31 ff., 68 ff. As Angus notes, mysticism is regarded by the great mystics not as a substitute for thought, but as the goal of intense concentration.

the most earnest lives of the time. The aim was to lose one's own consciousness and self, at least for a time, in the comprehensive divine.

Such a goal is totally different from both the Christian eschatology and the Christian experience of worship. The human centre of consciousness continues active and distinct in Christian worship and in the final divinely established order. It is not lost or minimized, but is rather preserved and enriched and given everlasting security. The New Testament offers no foothold for the idea of mystical absorption.

The only possible experience of a radically absorptive mystical kind of which any New Testament figure or writer can be accused is a temporary ecstasy in which the person loses consciousness, and the only person to consider is the Apostle Paul. He was caught up into the third heaven, but it was 'he' who was caught up, and he 'heard' things there (2 Cor. 12.4); there was no complete absorption even in this unique experience. He says that 'Christ lives in me' (Gal. 2.20), but he says in the same verse that he himself lives in the flesh at the same time that Christ lives in him; in other words, the living of Christ in him is not a cancellation of his personal consciousness. His letters attest abundantly that his Christian life was one of responsible personal existence. Led by the Spirit, he is still an individual man, and not an absorbed portion of the divine. Moreover, he has absolutely no idea that by his own spiritual exercises he can lift himself into communion or identification with the divine. Of his Christian life and privilege, he says that it is 'all the doing of God' (2 Cor. 5.18); even his faith is the gift of God (Eph. 2.8); his worship, even his prayers, are the utterance of the Spirit (Rom. 8.26); his acts are the fruit of the Spirit. But he continues to exist as an individual, infinitely indebted to God and ever led by the Spirit in the service of Christ his Lord. Not even Paul lives in the atmosphere of mystical absorption or mystical self-transformation.

9. One other tendency of the ancient world should be noticed.

Its religious life continually sought for effective techniques which would guarantee the benefits desired by the worshipper. The whole area of magic is an attempt by the worshipper to get his god under his control; the worshipper's aim is to make himself master of the situation; in its ultimate implication, this is self-deification.

Many and various were the forms of magic in ancient times.[32] With the crudest of them the Christian life under the Spirit's leading obviously had nothing in common. But there were more refined and attractive forms, ceremonies which when correctly observed were thought to guarantee the desired results. Such ceremonies were usually understood to have been prescribed by the god or gods. From then on things were in the hands of the believer. If he performed the external rite correctly, he was certain of the result.

We may dislike to use the word sacrament for this conception, but it is one way to regard a sacrament. What is important, however, is to see what the user of magic does and expects. By correct practice he supposedly has the god under control, or at least, on one view, an accepted priesthood does. The fertility cults so widely practised in the ancient world were based on the theory of sympathetic magic. The mystery cults, which in many cases grew out of the fertility cults, had in their usual observance at least remnants of the same conception.

The question is how far the Christian sacraments of baptism and the Lord's Supper were conceived in the New Testament to have this automatic effect based solely on correct observance of the rite.[33] The emphasis on faith and obedience and on the leading of the Spirit makes it certain that the main stream of the New Testament is not magical, nor is it corrupted by the idea of the automatic effectiveness of external rites correctly

---

[32] For a brief statement see Angus, *Religious Quests*, pp. 133 ff.

[33] Later Christians often resorted to magic, as many magical papyri prove; see M. P. Nilsson, *Die Religion in den griechischen Zauberpapyri*, 1948.

performed. If there was corruption, it was to a minor degree. Certainly Jesus himself cannot be accused of such corrupt sacramentalism. The intent and the heart were for him too important in all spiritual relations. The Apostolic Church shows no real support for the idea that God can be subdued or controlled by outward conformity or observance of any kind.

Upon occasion, Paul may suggest a magical idea. Baptism for the dead (1 Cor. 15.29) is so isolated and obscure a reference that we can make little of it,[34] and it is by no means certain that Paul shared the Corinthians' faith in its efficacy. Whenever he speaks of the result of the sacraments, he makes it clear that he does not think that the desired results follow automatically upon external performance of the rite. Indeed, he says the contrary. He says that the Israelites had the equivalent of our sacraments, but perished in the wilderness when they were disobedient (1 Cor. 10.1-5). Some Corinthians who have observed the sacraments have become sick and some have died because they have not lived in brotherly love in their common suppers (1 Cor. 11.30). In other words, Paul clearly denies that sacraments operate automatically.

The one place where magic is most nearly suggested in the New Testament is the sixth chapter of John, where eating the flesh and drinking the blood seem required and unconditionally effective (v. 54). But in the context the writer insists that it is the spirit which profits (v. 63), and it is a questionable exegesis which assigns to a sentence a meaning which is not that of the book as a whole and is immediately contradicted by the same author in the next paragraph.[35] This Gospel emphasizes so

---

[34] Concerning various proposed explanations, see A. Robertson and A. Plummer, *The First Epistle of St. Paul to the Corinthians*, 1911, *in loco*.

[35] E. C. Hoskyns, *The Fourth Gospel*, revised ed., edited by F. N. Davey, 1947, pp. 304 ff., deals with the interpretations which have been proposed. We are concerned here with the intent of the Gospel, which is to give the physical a subordinate but significant role in the Incarnation as well as in Christian worship and life. That this passage was later used to support magical conceptions is a fact.

much the centrality of believing that it is not reasonable to make its author an advocate of magic. We may convict him of loose expression, but not of trust in magic.

No, here, as throughout the New Testament, a life led by the Spirit has an inwardness, a vitality, a personal quality, a moral responsibility, which sets it apart from the realm of magic even when that magic is decked out in the attractive garb of allegedly sacramental observance. The Christian life roots in a historical career and in an understanding of that career through faith by the leading of the Holy Spirit. The widespread practice of magic in the Gentile world has not shaped the faith and form of life of the Church.

IV

Here, as before, we do well to listen to the voice of the ancient world. We may see many partial parallels with ancient life and thought, and as a result may wonder how much originality or difference the New Testament faith really had. The ancient world had no such problem. As far as I can find, they sensed the fact that the Gospel was a different thing from the religious messages which they had known. The Jews and later the Judaizers saw that it was breaking the limits of current Judaism. When attempts did begin to appropriate the new faith in the interests of some Gentile movement, as in Gnosticism, the Christians had the sound instinct to reject the danger.

At the start the sense of difference was present on both sides. And it should have been. The entire Christian Gospel centered in a historical person and career. God was known and interpreted in the light of that total career of Christ; he was 'The God and Father of our Lord Jesus Christ,' and on that basis is constructed an unsystematic but consistent New Testament theology. Christ was too great to be confined to a province and a generation; he came 'in the fullness of time' to do his central work, but all history finds its unity and interpretation through him. He sends the Spirit, and all of life, both in the Christian group and in the individuals who share the group life, is 'led by the Spirit,' whom he sends and who is linked with his career and nature and work.

This is indeed the Gospel of Christ the risen Lord. It is not in its essentials a secondary echo of themes originating elsewhere. It has the stamp of freshness, vitality, and originality. It is enough like the recurrent themes of human tradition so that it always invites comparison, and the similarities prove that it deals with the basic needs of men. But it is so unlike the alternative answers that its unique place cannot be denied by the historical student. One may ignore it, reject it, or accept it, but one cannot reasonably deny that it is a distinctive message which sets it against its environment.

INDEX OF BIBLICAL REFERENCES

Index of Biblical References

Index of Biblical References

INDEX OF AUTHORS